Bronwen Wallace

Essays on Her Works

T0019159

ESSENTIAL WRITERS SERIES 55

**Canada Council   Conseil des Arts
for the Arts   du Canada**

**ONTARIO ARTS COUNCIL
CONSEIL DES ARTS DE L'ONTARIO**

an Ontario government agency
un organisme du gouvernement de l'Ont

Guernica Editions Inc. acknowledges the support of the Canada Council
for the Arts and the Ontario Arts Council. The Ontario Arts Council
is an agency of the Government of Ontario.

We acknowledge the financial support of the Government of Canada.

Bronwen Wallace

Essays on Her Works

Edited by Wanda Campbell

**GUERNICA
EDITIONS**

TORONTO—BUFFALO—LANCASTER (U.K.)

2022

Guernica Founder: Antonio D'Alfonso

Wanda Campbell, editor
Michael Mirolla, general editor
Joseph Pivato, series editor
Cover and Interior Design: Errol F. Richardson
Cover Photo: Lisa Lowry, licensed under Creative Commons.

Guernica Editions Inc.
287 Templemead Drive, Hamilton (ON), Canada L8W 2W4
2250 Military Road, Tonawanda, N.Y. 14150-6000 U.S.A.
www.guernicaeditions.com

Distributors:
Independent Publishers Group (IPG)
600 North Pulaski Road, Chicago IL 60624
University of Toronto Press Distribution (UTP)
5201 Dufferin Street, Toronto (ON), Canada M3H 5T8
Gazelle Book Services, White Cross Mills
High Town, Lancaster LA1 4XS U.K.

First edition.
Printed in Canada.

Legal Deposit—Third Quarter
Library of Congress Catalog Card Number: 2022931783
Library and Archives Canada Cataloguing in Publication
Title: Bronwen Wallace : essays on her works / edited by Wanda Campbell.
Other titles: Bronwen Wallace (Guernica)
Names: Campbell, Wanda, 1963- editor.
Series: Essential writers series ; 55.
Description: Series statement: Essential writers series ; 55
Identifiers: Canadiana (print) 20220161992 | Canadiana (ebook) 20220172943 | ISBN
9781771837422 (softcover) | ISBN 9781771837439 (EPUB)
Subjects: LCSH: Wallace, Bronwen—Criticism and interpretation.
Classification: LCC PS8595.A56504 Z66 2022 | DDC C811/.54—dc23

*For my daughters Piper, Tilly, and Esme Bronwen
who are learning to invent themselves.*

Contents

Acknowledgements

I am grateful to all those who have contributed so generously to this collection with their critical and creative words, to Guernica Press for their continued efforts to provide resources on Canadian authors, to Joseph Pivato who first extended the invitation to embark on this journey and who has been a helpful guide along the way, to my home institution of Acadia University for granting me the time and resources to pursue this work, and to my family for ongoing support.

Susan Rudy and Aritha van Herk's essays first appeared in *Particular Arguments*, a special Bronwen Wallace issue of *Open Letter* (1991). Brenda Vellino's essay first appeared in *Postmodernism and the Ethical Subject* (2004). Patrick Lane's poem is from *Collected Poems of Patrick Lane* (Harbour Publishing 2011), Phil Hall's from *Killdeer: Essay-Poems* (Book*hug 2011), Phyllis Webb's from *Peacock Blue: Collected Poems* (Talonbooks 2014) and Jeremy Baxter's from *Common Magic: The Book of the New* (Artful Codger 2008), and all are reprinted with permission. All other essays are published here for the first time.

Abbreviations

All citations from Wallace's work throughout the volume are abbreviated as follows:

Poetry

MF	*Marrying into the Family* with *Bread and Chocolate* by Mary di Michele. Oberon, 1980.
SFT	*Signs of the Former Tenant*. Oberon, 1983.
CM	*Common Magic*. Oberon, 1985.
SPG	*The Stubborn Particulars of Grace*. McClelland & Stewart, 1987.
KCBB	*Keep That Candle Burning Bright*. Coach House, 1991.

Prose

PYT	*People You'd Trust Your Life To: Stories*. 1990. McClelland & Stewart, 2001.
AW	*Arguments with the World: Essays* edited by Joanne Page. Quarry, 1992.

Parenthetical references to texts elsewhere in this book are indicated by *supra* (above) or *infra* (below) with page numbers.

Wanda Campbell
Paying Attention: Wallace Now

> *Each site, a threshold*
> *into this slow discovery,*
> *the random testimony gathered*
> *as best we can, each of us down*
> *to essentials, as the failed are*
> *and the dead, who bear us forward*
> *in their fine, accurate arms.*
> "Testimonies" *The Stubborn Particulars of Grace* 49

Paying Attention

Just months before her death in 1989, Bronwen Wallace said, "If we are going to live with wholeness or integrity in the world, we have to pay attention to the particulars and politics of where we are" (*AW* 205). This she managed to do in five collections of poetry, *Marrying into the Family* (1980), *Signs of the Former Tenant* (1983), *Common Magic* (1985), *The Stubborn Particulars of Grace* (1987), and *Keep That Candle Burning Bright and Other Poems* (1990), a posthumously published short story collection *People You'd Trust Your Life To* (1990), and a collection of essays, interviews, and columns gathered in *Arguments with the World* (1992). She also produced two documentary films in collaboration with her partner Chris Whynot, *All You Have To Do* (1982) and *That's Why I'm Talking* (1984), and correspondence with Erin Mouré published in *Two Women Talking* (1993). This would be an extraordinary contribution under any circumstances but given the fact that Wallace did not publish her first poetry collection until she was 35 and died only nine years later, it is a truly remarkable achievement. I am hoping that this collection will help foster the critical and creative conversation regarding the many ways Wallace

5

paid attention to "the particulars and politics" of her world and invited us to do the same.

I first encountered Bronwen Wallace in the anthology *15 Canadian Poets X2* (1988) while I was an undergraduate. The seven poems by Wallace selected by editor Gary Geddes are still among my favourites, including "Common Magic," "Thinking with the Heart," and "A Simple Poem for Virginia Woolf" and Wallace's statements included in the "Notes on the Poets" resonated deeply with me as an aspiring writer and academic. Geddes later wrote that though he "found very little support for the inclusion of Bronwen's work" from either poets or academics, he was so impressed that he decided she should be included "both for the uniqueness of her voice and the unusually moving and uplifting content of her work" (391). Given her often dark subject matter, this assessment may be surprising, but as Peter Gzowski observed "there is something about [her] poetry that takes the curse off these things" (*AW* 24).

When I went on to do a Masters in Creative Writing at the University of Windsor, Wallace's presence was again in evidence since Windsor was one of the few places she lived outside of her hometown of Kingston, and Tom Wayman, the University of Windsor's Writer in Residence at the time, was instrumental in encouraging her writing career. While I was at Western completing my PhD, Bronwen Wallace served as Writer in Residence, and it was then that she learned of the cancer that caused her death at the age of 44. Even for those who were not in her inner circle, her belief that there was no such thing as ordinary had a tremendous impact. I learned so much from her work about being a writer, a woman, and a human being in magical and precarious times. When it came to a middle name for the youngest of my three daughters, it seemed fitting to choose the name of the poet who wrote poems about the common magic that flares like a match in the ordinary dark.

On the eve of the millennium when I had an opportunity to interview for a teaching position in Writing by Women at Acadia University where I still teach, I was tasked with developing a syllabus and choosing one woman writer to demonstrate how I would "teach" her work. The writer I chose was Wallace because after nearly a decade of teaching, I had repeatedly seen how students responded powerfully to her work, her activism, and her stubborn grace. When I gave a paper on why Wallace still matters at a conference at Mount Allison University in 2018, I was delighted to accept an invitation from Guernica editor, Joseph Pivato, to edit this collection of essays on her work.

Typically, I wouldn't mention personal details in an academic work, but Wallace gave us permission to do so because, as she explains in "One More Woman Talking" included in this volume, she was interested in "trying to see how the unique and private anecdotes became part of a story that gave each of our lives a public and collective meaning" (37 *infra*). Though there are scholars and writers who continue to believe strongly in her work, including Carolyn Smart who has worked tirelessly to bring out the *Collected Poems of Bronwen Wallace* (2020), there have been those who questioned Wallace's poetry, her politics, or the praise she continued to garner from those she inspired. In his memoir, *The Names of Things* (2006), David Helwig writes:

> Sometimes it seemed that in her last days Bron, dying so prematurely, was becoming to her friends and guardians, a kind of feminist saint and martyr, and the fervour of those who were committed to seeing her through was not always discriminating [....] Bronwen greatly deserved loyalty and care, but zealous enthusiasm is always a dangerous thing. (214)

Rhea Tregebov who includes a selection of Wallace's poetry in *Sudden Miracles: Eight Women Poets* (1991) put it this way:

> Since her death, we dwell on her remarkable generosity of spirit, often forgetting what a ferocious, and sometimes difficult, friend she was. But that fierceness and stubbornness—the side not often referred to—were an important aspect of the talent that drove Wallace to go so far so fast in her writing, and to stick to the stubborn heart of things. (29)

Rereading Wallace's poetry and prose more than three decades after it was written, I am reassured by how relevant it still feels, and this gathering of essays and poetic responses will, I hope, reveal in various ways why this is so.

The work of Bronwen Wallace deserves reconsideration for the ways it crystallizes many of the themes that emerge throughout the 1970s and 1980s. According to Shelley Martin, "Though we can roughly place Wallace within the Second Wave along a feminist timeline, she also recognizes and embraces the ways in which feminism was evolving" (63). In one of her many columns for the *Kingston Whig-Standard*, later published in *Arguments with the World*, Wallace writes:

> Listening to bell hooks reminded me that I cannot always rest with the sometimes-comforting experience of exploring what I share with other white, middle-class feminists. I have a lot to learn yet and to learn it I must enter the harder, more complex regions where women's experience begins to diverge and differ. I believe such journeys are necessary in order that that imagined world may become possible and whole—for all of us. (*AW* 48)

Like many women writers before her, Wallace calls for acknowledgement of the female experience and celebrates the lives of girls and women, as does Alice Munro whose work she admired. Like Virginia Woolf before her, Wallace saw her task as filling gaps in the record of human experience: "I see myself as a feminist writer whose job it is to explore what our culture has previously silenced" (*AW* 72). Of her first book of poems, *Marrying into the Family* published in 1980 alongside Mary di Michele's *Bread and Chocolate*, she said, "I began to write the poems in the first place because I was struck by how little I knew about any of my female ancestors" (*AW* 150). Exploring that absence became part of the project which would lead her down the road of recovery, in both senses of the word. "For Wallace," argues Donna Bennett, "the past is a necessary part of our experience of the present and of our future actions" (67).

In *A Room of One's Own*, Woolf wrote, "All these infinitely obscure lives remain to be recorded" (85) and Wallace concurred: "For you, as a reader, it means lots of poems and stories about battles, but very few about raising children. Half of the story of what we are, as a species, is missing" (*AW* 108). She was concerned about the real-world implications of this imbalance for both women and men. In a column entitled "English Literature: It's Still a Man's World," she reflects on her son's school reading list which, in the 1980's, included hardly any women at all:

> And so, my son will read little by women this year. This absence will teach him a great deal. It will teach him that human experience is the same as male experience. Therefore, he doesn't need to question how he sees things. It will teach him that the experience of women is not something he can learn from. Therefore, he doesn't need to listen when women speak or believe what he hears us say. (*AW* 182)

If men and women see only the images of themselves offered up by literary and popular culture, rather than the far more complex and nuanced reality we are, she concludes, in big trouble.

In one of her most anthologized poems, "A Simple Poem for Virginia Woolf," Wallace implies that there are no simple solutions to the diverse challenges of women's lives. She had wanted to write a simple poem "separating the words / from the lives they come from" (*SFT* 50), a poem as "simple / and perfectly round / hard as an / egg I thought / only once I'd said egg / I thought of the smell / of bacon grease and dirty frying-pans / and whether there were enough for breakfast / I couldn't help it" (*SFT* 48). Before she is a baker's dozen lines into her poem, it becomes "tangled," "confessional," and filled with excuses she did not mean to make, details she did not mean to mention, stories she did not mean to tell. Inevitably, the poem becomes as rich and ragged as her own life. By the end of the poem she confesses that "countless gritty details [...] intervene / between the poem I meant to write / and this one" (*SFT* 51). Women she knows and women she doesn't "press around [her] / waiting their turn" (*SFT* 51). The word "turn" is a superb choice for the closing word of this poem because it means, of course, the chance to speak in succession, but it also means revolution, melodic ornament, and stroll. These silenced women await the chance to walk out of their rooms and into the world and back into their rooms to record the wonder of what they see. Like Woolf, Wallace speaks on behalf of those who have been silenced and prevented, those who have been locked out and locked in.

In *A Room of One's Own*, Woolf admits to "glancing with envy at the reader next door who was making the neatest abstracts, headed often with an A or a B or a C, while [her] own notebook rioted with the wildest scribble of contradictory jottings" (30-31). Wallace similarly finds that writing, especially writing about women, is not a straightforward enterprise: In his explanation of her approach, Geddes quotes Wallace: "The poem never goes from A to B to C as I thought it would. I discover it as I go," then continues:

As a keeper of the stories, Wallace has mastered the so-called digression, or lateral shift, so common to the tradition of oral story-telling, wherein the narrator appears to have forgotten or abandoned the main story momentarily, but has, in effect, deepened the narrative by bringing new material to bear. (Geddes *15 Canadian Poets X2* 566)

As Wallace herself put it, "Some of what happens in my poems is an attempt to capture how women's conversations work, which is never linear but circles and moves around things" (*AW* 202). According to Tregebov, her mature work "spirals outward in accordance with the basically expansive nature of Wallace's impulse which is to include and include and include" (30).

Another of Wallace's stated goals was **accessibility**, to make her poems like "kitchen-table talk" tied to an oral tradition that reflects women's conversations, circular, digressive, open to interruptions and healing gestures which Bennett describes as "stream-of-conversation poems" (71). Sharing many of the elements of oral storytelling, her narratives almost always make use of the familiar "you." Wallace wanted her poetry to be accessible not only to scholars, but also to everyday people. She was just as likely to find wisdom in the tabloids as in the classics. One of her last poems, "Miracles," begins with an epigraph by a woman who owns a velvet painting of Elvis that weeps real tears: "*Sometimes I don't know whether to be grateful or terrified*" (*KCBB* 53). This is not to suggest that her work is simple or unlayered, but that it is "polyphonic" as Susan Glickman argues elsewhere in this volume, and peripatetic: "The poems aren't about what happens but about what's discovered. The narratives in my poems are like guide posts towards a mystery at the centre of any story, the mystery of our existence or the mystery of our personality" (*AW* 210). Wallace offers us an alchemy that transmutes the mundane into gold in moments "when you realize that magic / is not the trick itself / but the magician's hardworked skill / with coins and handkerchiefs / the complex possibilities / of common things" (*SFT* 101).

The magic may be "common," but we still might miss it through a lack of **attention**. Wallace not only challenges us to "pay attention to the particulars and politics of where we are" (*AW* 205) but provides us with "smaller stratagems" (*SPG* 33) for doing so, a process we can trace in the poem "Thinking with the Heart" (*CM* 59-62). Firstly, acknowledge others who also fight the good fight. As she so often does, Wallace dedicates her poem to a woman who is important to her, in this case fellow poet Mary di Michele. Acknowledging her female friends has always been important to Wallace:

> It's through my women friends that I survive. It's not that these relationships are 'better than' those I share with my lover, my son, or my male friends. It's just that they're absolutely necessary to my survival. Period…. We're speaking with the authority of female human beings. As a poet I couldn't do this without Mary and the others. One more snide, time-warp, patently sexist review and I'd probably quit. But because I see us as a group, I am able to appreciate and work on my own strengths as a writer. (Wallace qtd. by Billings 141)

Secondly, make the subject as accessible as possible, even if it means adopting a different perspective, as suggested in the epigraph from photographer Diane Arbus: "*I work from awkwardness. By that I mean I don't like to arrange things. If I stand in front of something, instead of arranging it, I arrange myself*" (*CM* 59). Then you pay attention to everyone on all sides of the debate, including the policeman who doesn't understand why a victim of domestic abuse would refuse to charge her abuser: "*The problem with you women is, you think with your heart*" (*CM* 59). Like other poems based on Wallace's work at Interval House, the Kingston shelter for battered women, this poem reveals the dangers of failing to understand one another's challenges and choices. Discussing this poem with Peter

Gzowski, Wallace admitted that at first she thought "anybody who stayed in that situation was an idiot" (*AW* 22), but then through really paying attention and really listening she began to see "that there are so many factors in even the SMALLEST choice that it isn't easy" (*AW* 23). Ultimately, we must reunite the head and the heart while admitting our damage and using it to empower rather than undermine.

> But right now, the policeman's waiting
> for the woman to decide.
> That's how he thinks of it; *choice*
> or how you can always get what you want
> if you want it badly enough.
> Everything else he ignores,
> like the grip of his own heart's red
> persistent warning that he too is fragile.
> He thinks he thinks with his brain […]
> And when he thinks like that
> he loses himself forever. (*CM* 61)

The only rooms we can really call our own, argues Wallace, are the four chambers of our heart, and we must learn to name what lives there before we can love anything at all.

> I'm writing to the wounded part of each person, men as well as women. The power of feminism is the power of the victim who has learned a way to use her damage. There's a great line in an Adrienne Rich poem about knowing that her wound came from the same place as her power. When you get in touch with your damage, recognize and care for it, you also discover the source of your power. We know that abusers, men who batter, or anybody who abuses children, have usually been abused themselves and have denied it. It's the denial

of our damage, our limitations, our vulnerability, our mortality that's got us where we are. (*AW* 210)

Wallace's allusion to the poem "Power" in which Adrienne Rich explains that Marie Curie's wounds (radiation sickness) came from the same source as her power (the scientific brilliance that gave her a place in history) suggests that denying one's damage can be dangerous.

Paying attention is vital, but it is not enough. Throughout her work, Wallace calls for **action**, and the call is urgent. "In using female anecdote as a metaphor for human experience, I see myself in a simple way assuming that a female view of the world could be a human view of the world. Underneath that is the belief that, if we don't listen to this voice, we're not going to be here to have any view of the world" (*AW* 208). In a column entitled "Women's Week 'With Courage and Vision,'" Wallace again alludes to Adrienne Rich in her assertion that "we progress as a species because of the small acts of people who don't make it to the history books" (*AW* 112). If the goal of telling women's stories "is to effect political change by revising the social and cultural attitudes that devalue both the stories and the women who live them" (Martin 61), Wallace repeatedly emphasized the need for choice and change. "I think the main message is that we're not totally the victims of our society or the victims of our past or the victims of our biology or anything else. That we can choose, that we can make changes" (*AW* 23). In her contribution to this volume, Brenda Vellino explores how Wallace provides a model for ethical humility by tracing in her poems a sequence from hearing, to seeing, to doing, "undertaking urgent action based on our intimate connection" (106 *infra*).

In her final public appearance, a keynote address to a large audience on International Women's Day just days after she was diagnosed with cancer, Wallace said this:

When we look at what we're up against in global terms, it sometimes seems impossible that anything can change. And yet one of the reasons we are all here today is that we know, as individual women, in our own particular lives, that change is possible—individual change and collective change. It seems to me that feminism, as a political force in this culture, is one of the main agents for social change at this time, specifically because it connects the individual and the collective, the private and the political. (*AW* 224)

Wallace maintains that theory without engagement is insufficient. In correspondence with Erin Mouré, Wallace wrote:

We must begin with what we are, with what we have already learned, with how we have acted and continue to act in the world, as well as from theory. At least, I must, I feel, if I am to continue to address the women I know who are acting in the world. (*Two Women Talking* 23-24).

According to di Michele, all of Wallace's "writing is imbued with energy and love and faith which enables you to do things" (qtd. by Martin 70). In her final collection *Keep that Candle Burning Bright*, Wallace encourages in us the capacity for wonder, and the desire to do. Even when "we don't know whether to be grateful or terrified" (*KCBB* 53), we need to reach out to one another with acknowledgement, attention, and action. Ultimately, the willingness to act does not have to come from a place of perfection but rather from a place of purpose. As Wallace says in "This is the Closest I Come to a Song":

Why not sing for what we can't do, instead of all this booming and bragging, most of us stuck in the back row anyway, squawking, gimped-up. What if some tuneless wonder's all we've got to say for ourselves? Off-key, our failings held out, at last, to each other. What else have we got to offer, really? What else do we think they're for? (*KCBB* 32)

In her final poem entitled "Miracles," Wallace reminds us that "it's centuries since the word / *mirari*, to wonder at, began to blur / through the French *mirer*, into *mirare*, / to regard intently" (*KCBB* 55). I will be forever grateful to Wallace for reversing this blur in me.

Surprisingly, with the one exception of *The Stubborn Particulars of Grace*, none of Wallace's poetry collections contain a Table of Contents. I have never seen any explanation of what I assume was a considered choice, but it always struck me as one of the peculiar pleasures of her work. I consider the Table of Contents for a poetry collection akin to the table of appetizers at a party, a place where the shy can stand to fortify themselves before plunging into the fauvist river of human speech, but with Wallace, as I put it once in a poem, "I have no choice but to venture / and wait for her to whisk gracefully by / with dazzling silver trays of / delicacies all the more delicious / because I did not see them coming."

Wallace Now

In an article that first appeared in *The Globe and Mail* on August 26, 1989, the day after her death, Dennis Lee acknowledged Wallace's unique and remarkable contribution; "in poetry, be it Canadian or international, no one else had even tried some of the things she was doing" (13). And yet, the critical response is surprisingly sparse. According to Susan Rudy and Eric Savoy, the editors of the special 1991 *Open Letter* issue dedicated to Wallace's work in which Lee's article was reprinted as "A Geography of Stories," "her work has received little academic recognition" (5) and not much has changed in the intervening years. I have done my best in this collection to acknowledge the key contributors to the critical conversation over the years and add some new voices. It is no accident that so many of the contributors to this volume are writers as well as academics and teachers, since Wallace has been an inspiration in both realms.

As we trace some milestones in relation to her work, from the time of her death until now, we see how her voice continues to be relevant. As Anita Lahey points out in a 2020 article in the *Walrus* entitled "Poetic Justice," Wallace's poems "ring powerfully amidst the #MeToo movement" (63). Following a brief biography which situates Wallace within the "particulars" of the various "countries" in which she lived, we hear from Wallace herself in "One More Woman Talking" (1987) in a statement that appeared first in Rhea Tregebov's *Sudden Miracles: Eight Women Poets* (1991) and later in *Two Women Talking, Correspondence, 1985 to 1987* (1993) edited by Susan McMaster in the *Living Archives* of The Feminist Caucus of The League of Canadian Poets.

Wallace gave several fine interviews in the last decade of her life as listed in the Bibliography at the end of this volume, including one with Peter Gzowski and one with Janice Williamson which both appeared in the 1991 issue of *Open Letter* dedicated to Wallace and later in *Arguments with the World* (1992). A less available interview is one with Barbara Cantar that took place at Queen's University on November 2, 1987 and first appeared in *Arc* magazine. Wallace explores many of the themes that permeate her work and discusses the role of geography, autobiography, family, her time at the women's shelter, the canon, feminism, literary influences and the political nature of art. Wallace responds to Cantar's final question, "Where does the artist fit into changing society, the world?" by quoting Gabriel García Márquez: "I do that by writing as well as I can" (59 *infra*). In *The Fragrance of Guava*, García Márquez writes:

> Many of my militant friends who so often feel the need to dictate to writers what they should or should not write are, unconsciously perhaps, taking a reactionary stance inasmuch as they are imposing restrictions on creative freedom. I believe a novel about love is as valid as any other. When it comes down to it, the writer's duty—his revolutionary duty if you like—is to write well. (59)

Wallace has indeed written well, revising "endlessly" in the six books she produced in nine years and, as the Cantar interview reveals, what may appear casual is the result of considerable craft.

The essays begin appropriately with a reflection by Mary di Michele whose poems were published alongside Wallace's very first collection, in 1985. In her epigraph, di Michele draws attention to Wallace's affinity for Woolf. As Elizabeth Greene points out in her introduction to *Common Magic: The Book of the New,* a large picture of Woolf hung in Wallace's study (9) and anyone who has read "A Simple Poem for Virginia Woolf" cannot doubt the debt that Wallace felt she owed, though she did acknowledge that "Even Virginia Woolf's form did not redeem all of her content, which is often class-biased and hidebound" (*Two Women Talking* 23). By drawing parallels between the birds of Byzantium in the poems of W.B. Yeats and the singing parrot in the Caribou Hotel in Carcross, N.W.T, in Wallace's poem "Testimonies" (*SPG* 47), di Michele explores the distinction between art and artifice and grapples with what will ultimately endure. I am grateful to di Michele for granting permission to also reprint "Angel of Slapstick," her elegy for her friend that first appeared as the final poem in *Luminous Emergencies* (1990), a collection that di Michele dedicated to Wallace, "*la meilleure, ma soeur.*" This dedication is followed by an epigraph from John Berger's *And Our Faces, My Heart, Brief as Photos,* "the past grows gradually around one, like a placenta for dying" (78), a phrase that is transformed by Wallace into "placenta for my future" in reference to the names of local weeds and local words, "these stories, all I have to call a county" (*CM* 16) in her poem "Distance from Harrowsmith to Tamworth."

In conversation with Barbara Godard, di Michele talks about "Angel of Slapstick" as "the most comprehensive of what I feel for her, and what I am as a writer and what I am because of what I've learned from her [....] I was getting a sense of all that she could bring together in a poem which was the way I remember her teaching me how to make soup" (48). In that same conversation, di Michele notes Berger's influence on Wallace: "it's Berger's whole sense of language addressing the wound, that was Bron's, one of her major concerns" (46). At the heart of "Angel of Slapstick" is a quotation from Berger's *And Our Faces, My Heart, Brief as Photos* which reads in full:

> Poetry's impulse to use metaphor, to discover resemblance, is not to make comparisons (all comparisons as such are hierarchical) or to diminish the particularity of any event; it is to discover those correspondences of which the sum total would be proof of the indivisible totality of existence. To this totality poetry appeals, and its appeal is the opposite of a sentimental one; sentimentality always pleads for an exemption, for something which is divisible. Apart from reassembling by metaphor, poetry rewrites by its reach. It equates the reach of a feeling with the *reach* of the universe... (96-97)

The quotation that closes the poem *"this gentleness we learn / from what we can't heal"* is from Wallace's poem "What it Comes to Mean" (*CM* 77). In addition to what it reveals about the method of making poems being explored by these two poets and friends, the title "Angel of Slapstick" hints at Wallace's sense of humour which is often noted in remembrance but rarely in the critical record, though Wallace freely admitted "I like to make people laugh" (*AW* 213) and described humour as "another way of trying to set up some sort of openness between the reader and the speaker" (*AW* 213). As Mary di Michele put it in *Anything is Possible: A Selection of Eleven Women Poets*: "How can I ever thank Bronwen Wallace enough for her intelligence, her enlightenment, her courage? I'm in awe of this woman who has such adult assurance and knowledge, with a child's sense of play, of fun" (9).

There were many tributes published in newspapers and literary journals after Wallace's death, as well as several fine reviews of individual works and theses written at the undergraduate, graduate and doctoral levels, as listed in the Selected Bibliography, but the critical conversation took a great leap forward in 1991 with "Particular Arguments: A Special Issue On Bronwen Wallace" in *Open Letter*, edited by Susan Rudy [then Rudy Dorscht] and Eric Savoy. Anyone interested in Wallace's work should read this collection of essays in its entirety, since it remains, to date, the most extended critical assessment of Wallace's work. Included are the interviews already noted as well as the conversation between Mary di Michele and Barbara Godard, poems by Erin Mouré and Phyllis Webb, and essays by Aritha van Herk, J.M. Kertzer, Eric Savoy, Bina Freiwald and the two editors, Eric Savoy and Susan Rudy who draw attention to what was and remains important about Wallace's work: "Wallace's work impresses us because of its interrogation of representation, its critique of patriarchal ideology, its call for social change, and its insistence on the strength of women's voices" (5).

I am pleased to include Susan Rudy's essay from that issue with a new introduction in which she explains how Wallace influenced her understanding of gender "ontoformativity." Rudy's acknowledgement that Wallace "wouldn't have used the term" (76 *infra*) echoes a passage from "Lillian on the Inside," the final story in the new edition of *People You'd Trust Your Life To* in which Lillian reflects on the content of the conversations she has with her daughter Lisa and her partner Angie: "Feminist topics, she guessed though the word 'feminist' felt odd in her mouth, like the taste of mango or kiwi or some other exotic fruit she only ate in restaurants. With Lisa and Angie, it was like they ate that fruit everyday" (*PYT* 208). Even before Wallace knew the words or they still "felt odd" in her mouth, she was pointing the way to a deeper understanding of progressive ideas. As Donna Bennett put it in her article published in 1991, "Bronwen Wallace was for Canadian readers and writers and particularly for women poets of her generation, a Wise Woman. She told us things we were not yet able to see. She opened up her life to let us learn about ourselves" (77).

The following year marked another milestone in Wallace scholarship with the publication of her prose in *Arguments with the World: Essays by Bronwen Wallace* (1992), including her columns in the *Kingston Whig-Standard* from 1987 to 1989, various interviews and essays, and the text from her final public appearance, "Blueprints for a Larger Life." In her Foreword to this invaluable resource, Joanne Page writes "Bronwen's voice resonates like a struck bell through the issues of her day, issues still ours" (*AW* 7).

Two years later, in 1994, *The Bronwen Wallace Award for Emerging Writers* was created by Wallace's literary executor Carolyn Smart with the following criteria as listed on the website: "Bronwen Wallace felt that young writers should have more opportunities for greater recognition early in their careers, and so this annual award is given to a writer below the age of 35 who has published poetry or prose in a literary magazine or anthology, but has not yet been published in book form and is without a book contract." Reflecting on the importance of this award many years later, its inaugural recipient, Michael Crummey said:

I had friends who were starting out as writers who called Bronwen Wallace up cold—out of the blue—just to ask her if she would look at their work. And she never said no to those people. But I was pretty deeply closeted as a writer at the time and also, I think too shy of a person to approach her directly that way. But I do feel like, belatedly, I have benefited from Bronwen's generosity and her spirit through my association with this award. I think the Bronwen Wallace Award is one of, if not the most important, awards for young writers in Canada. It carries on the work that Bronwen did mentoring and encouraging young writers. (Crummey *YouTube*)

Wallace's efforts with young writers, as well as her columns and speeches, all draw attention to her ethical engagement with the world, and ethical engagement is at the heart of Brenda Vellino's essay first published in *Postmodernism and the Ethical Subject* (2004) but substantially revised for this volume. According to Vellino, "Wallace reanimates former categories of subjectivity, agency, community and, most importantly, ethics. Her attentiveness to complex registers of identity, contexts, and construction of knowledge/power indicates implicit incorporation of some of postmodernism's important questions" (113 *infra*). Vellino sees Wallace's ethical engagement as a call to action on behalf of all who share this planet.

Next is Patrick Lane's elegy "For Bronwen Wallace" that first appeared in his *Last Water Song* (2007) in a series of thirteen elegies for writers that included five other women, Adele Wiseman, Anne Szumigalski, Elizabeth Smart, Gwendolyn MacEwen, and Pat Lowther. The note to those elegies which appear again in *The Collected Poems of Patrick Lane* (2011) edited by Russell Brown and Donna Bennett reads, "each contains allusions to the work of the poet being addressed" (535). The line *There's only so much anyone can say* is the opening line of Wallace's poem "Splitting It Up" (*CM* 66) and *we carry our lives in our hands* is from "Learning from the Hands" (*CM* 87). *The cadence in a woman's voice* is also italicized in the first published version of the poem, perhaps in allusion to "As the cadence of an old woman's voice / becomes the line that will lead others / into the territory her people saw" ("Testimonies" *SPG* 47), and the final line "like a tree fallen in a forest no one hears" has disappeared in the version that appears in the *Collected Poems* which is reprinted here. This tribute from one poet to another whose work bears a certain resemblance is significant because it reveals, like Phil Hall's poem "Twenty Lost Years," that Wallace's influence was felt well beyond the female community. Wallace spoke of learning from women writers such as Margaret Atwood, Dorothy Livesay, P.K. Page, Elizabeth Brewster, Alice Munro and Flannery O'Connor, but also from men such as Al Purdy and others: "If I think of the male writers I admire, such as Galway Kinnell or Philip Levine or Pat Lane, there is that same attention to everyday things" (Meyer 103). Though the scholarship on Wallace has mainly been written by women, there have been male scholars writing about her work, most notably Eric Savoy who co-edited the special edition of *Open Letter* with Susan Rudy, J.M. Kertzer, and Stephen Scobie, but poems by her male contemporaries are also testament to the wider reach of her work.

In 2008, a conference entitled *Common Magic* was organized in Kingston to celebrate Wallace's legacy, with over fifty contributors including family members, authors, and scholars. Fifteen presentations made at the Conference by Ron Baxter, Chris Whynot, Jeremy Baxter, Shelagh Rogers, Lorna Crozier and others were made into podcasts which, as of 2022, are still available online. This unprecedented gathering revealed the ongoing relevance and influence of Wallace's work, but also marked the creation of the Wallace fonds at Queen's University. Material ranging from 1978 to 1997 including correspondence, journals, notebooks, and reviews held by Carolyn Smart, then turned over to Wallace's son, was brought to Queen's University Archives, with the assistance of Joanne Page, in conjunction with the conference.

For more information see http://db-archives.library.queensu.ca/index.php/bronwen-wallace-fonds.

One of those to present at that conference was Lorraine York. In her paper "'Crazy Detours': The Digressive Activism of Bronwen Wallace," she identifies "digression as a major mode in which Wallace writes activist poetry" (121 *infra*). Many critics have commented on the prevalence of detours and double backs in Wallace's work, but York explores *pentimento* which she describes as "a painterly change of heart" as a particularly "suggestive analogue" for what Wallace achieves as an activist poet (127 *infra*) by opening everything to examination.

"Family, politics, work, landscape: she had all the ingredients," writes Joanne Page in her Foreword to *Arguments with the World*; "With encouragement from the poet Phil Hall, Bronwen began to find her distinctive literary voice" (8). The "essay-poem" included here, "Twenty Lost Years: The Evolution of Bronwen Wallace's Voice," which Hall first presented at the 2008 conference later appeared in *Killdeer: Essay-Poems* (Book*hug 2011), a collection that went on to win the 2011 Governor General's Literary Award for Poetry and the 2012 Trillium Book Award. In an echo of Wallace's own style, "*the jumble we just can't throw out*" (155 *infra*), Hall combines quotations from authors as various as Marshall McLuhan and Mikhail Bakhtin, snippets of politics and popular culture, reflections, memories, anecdotes, and strange details, like the fact that Sigmund Freud and Ivan Illich also died of cancer of the mouth. Glimpses of Wallace's evolving poetics shine forth: "she can't tell the story without telling how it is being told" (155 *infra*) and the whole is laced with Hall's admiration for Wallace and grief for her loss because of all she had to offer including "a unified front against despair" (148 *infra*) and a talent "for weaving disparate types into community" (156 *infra*).

Another writer who presented at the *Common Magic* conference was Susan Glickman, and her paper "Angels, Not Polarities" is included here. Glickman wrestles with "why Bronwen Wallace, a poet who repeatedly insisted that she had no interest in writing fiction, ultimately found herself doing so" (131 *infra*) by exploring Wallace's love for narrative at the heart of each genre. Glickman argues that while feminism strongly influenced the content of the poetry of those who grew up in the 60s and 70s, "it had a more radical effect on Bronwen Wallace: it was the source of her poetic *form*. Not only did she address the subject of women's lives, she told it in women's voices—and in the typical style of women's conversations" (133 *infra*).

Understandably, what little criticism there is regarding Wallace's work focuses on her poetry, though there have been discussions of individual stories like Janice Kulyk Keefer's article on "The Scuba Diver in Repose," or on a particular motif, like Danielle Schaub's exploration of alcohol in Wallace's fiction. Aritha van Herk's "Ghost Narratives: A Haunting," however, deals with Wallace's entire short story collection, so I am pleased to include it in this volume. In her essay which first appeared in the special Wallace issue of *Open Letter* in 1992, van Herk explores how Wallace's stories defy conventional narrative patterns or plots because they are haunted by stories that are unrestrained, forbidden, intuited, doubled, or captured in some other form such as photographs and emanations. Both Wallace's characters and her readers are left asking, "What story is the story trying to tell us?" But as van Herk so eloquently puts it, "They traverse the countries of each others' futures: and they know the secrets and the hauntings of their inside lives. These are the people you can trust your life / story to" (172 *infra*).

There has not been much in the way of recent scholarship on Wallace other than a chapter entitled "Feminism, Motherhood, and Possibilities in the Writing of Bronwen Wallace" by Shelley Martin published in *Feminist Mothering* (2008). Significantly, however, in 2016 and 2017 Wallace's work was translated into

French for the first time with *Lieu des origines: poèmes choisis, traduits et présentés par Isabelle Miron avec la collaboration d'Éric Bergeron* (Noroît 2016) and *Si c'est ça l'amour* (Les Allusifs 2017) translated by René-Daniel Dubois. Miron's collection named for "Place of Origin," a poem from *Common Magic* (11-13), contains French translations of 31 poems from *Signs of the Former Tenant, Common Magic,* and *The Stubborn Particulars of Grace,* and an *Afterword* by Erin Mouré. In her introduction, Miron writes: "*tous ces poèmes, c'est son legs d'amour à l'humanité*" (8). Wallace's "legacy of love to humanity" will now be accessible to a wider audience because of these translations of poems which, as Erin Mouré puts it in her Afterword, "*résonnent pour nous à travers le temps*" (91), resonate for us through time.

The Québécois playwright René-Daniel Dubois, who has also translated Timothy Findley, named his translated collection of Wallace's short stories *Si c'est ça l'amour* after the story "If This is Love" rather than *People You'd Trust Your Life To* which he translates as *Ces êtres à qui l'on confierait sa vie.* In an interview in *La Presse* on 26 March 2017, Dubois highlights the "beautiful" attention Wallace pays to her characters without judging them but admits that the "silences" were difficult to translate: "*C'est entre les lignes que ça se passe, pas tant dans ce qui est dit que dans cette espèce de tension qui finit par apparaître. C'est écrit très simplement, puis tout à coup un trou s'ouvre en dedans de soi quand on lit. Arriver à rendre ça en français, ç'a été un beau défi.* [It's between the lines that it's happening, not so much in what is said as in this kind of tension that finally appears. It is written very simply, then suddenly a hole opens inside oneself when one reads. To be able to do that in French, it was a beautiful challenge.]

I have attempted in my own contribution to this volume to examine how a single motif, the body as map, permeates both Wallace's poetry and prose, allowing us to consider Flannery O'Connor's statement that "Possibility and limitation mean about the same thing" in the light of "the power of the female understanding of the body as a limit we can love..." (Wallace, *Two Women Talking* 22).

Phyllis Webb's poem "Bronwen's Earrings" speaks to Wallace's physical presence, and in particular her ears; by highlighting the "hilarious light on the lure / of the pierced ear" (192 *infra*), Webb draws attention to Wallace's capacity to listen, a practice which is at the heart of both her poetics and her politics. It is worth noting here that the word "hilarious" which came to mean "exceedingly amusing" in the 1920s, is from the Greek *hilaros* meaning "cheerful." The words Wallace lured to herself "need to be heard;" like the "wild bird" adorning her ear in the photograph on the cover of this volume, they invite flight. In Webb's poem "someone crosses / a street in Kingston / picking up flute notes" and in Wallace's poem, "A Stubborn Grace," our own dying gathers us up until "the last notes drop / into the still pools / the song has made in each of us" (*SFT* 106).

Various scholars have discovered tools to contextualize and clarify Wallace's work in her correspondence with Erin Mouré as preserved in *Two Women Talking* (1993). In her foreword to this chapbook of letters, Erin Mouré wrote:

> These texts mark a particular historical moment, and in reading them you will eavesdrop on that moment, between 1985 and 1987, when the Bronwen Wallace and Erin Mouré of that time pursued together a discussion of feminist theory. The two paths of their discussing, their crossing, their incessant explaining, objecting, tripping, excitability, is part of the process of thinking itself—which is dynamic, which requires the community of others... and can only occur with respect and caring, a willingness to state emphatically, but also to listen... (*Two Women Talking* 9)

Their exchange is the subject of Andrea Beverley's contribution to this volume. As a younger scholar she brings a fresh perspective on the interdisciplinarity and enduring relevance of Wallace's writing. Her chapter also reveals the wonderful pedagogical potential of Wallace's complete oeuvre which rings true to my own experience of teaching her work over the years, and which echoes the many affirmations of Wallace's own considerable gifts as a teacher. Beverley maintains: "For the poetic speaker, and for Wallace writing, conversation between women sparks poetic creation. Stories inspire, render possible, and sustain the explorations and musings that comprise the poetry" (195 *infra*).

A momentous milestone in Wallace scholarship was the publication in 2020 of Carolyn Smart's *Collected Poems of Bronwen Wallace* (McGill-Queen's UP) which includes Wallace's published poetry much of which was no longer in print, some early unpublished poems, an introduction, extensive notes, and a bibliography, all of which will foster and facilitate the ongoing conversation about her work. Smart, who was hired to replace Wallace to teach creative writing at Queen's University, has done much to keep the memory of her friend alive over the years, including founding the RBC Bronwen Wallace Award and editing the long-awaited *Collected Poems*. Smart, who met her husband through a blind date organized by Wallace and who regarded her as close friend, mentor, editor, and role model, continues to contribute significantly to the project of preserving her voice, noting that it feels as if the conversation carries on between them. As she says in her poem "October" from *The Way to Come Home* (1992): "I am learning anew / to release all I cannot hold, / these moments of luminous grace."

Another individual who has been instrumental in keeping Wallace's memory alive is her son and literary executor Jeremy Baxter who is featured in several poems including "My Son is Learning to Invent" (*CM* 17-19) and "Jeremy at Ten" (*CM*

82-84). In response to an invitation to be included in this project, he wrote: "I am continually pleased and of course somewhat proud that people are still reading and conversing about my mom's work." I am delighted to conclude this collection with his poem "Remembering in Blue" which first appeared in *Common Magic: The Book of the New* (2008) and is reprinted here with permission.

Which brings us to Wallace now. W.B. Yeats once asked, "How can the arts overcome the slow dying of men's hearts that we call the progress of the world?" (200). In part, by allowing us to hear one another's stories and women, insists Wallace, must be included in the telling: "When we tell people intimate things about ourselves, we are in some way asking for support, inclusion, something, a healing gesture from the other person" (*AW* 213). It is my sincere desire that through the words gathered here, scholars, teachers, writers and readers will be aided in their efforts to continue the conversation. As Wallace herself says in "One More Woman Talking" included in this volume:

> What I hear in "ordinary conversation" is that movement that goes on among us when we feel safe enough or confident enough or loved enough to explore the power within us, that power which is so often belittled or denied by the society around us (or by ourselves), though it remains the power by which, in our best moments, we manage to survive and to live, sometimes, with grace. (38-39 *infra*)

Works Cited

Arbus, Diane. *Diane Arbus*. Aperture, 1972.

Bennett, Donna. "Bronwen Wallace and the Meditative Poem." *Queen's Quarterly*. vol. 98, no.1, 1991, pp.58-79.

Berger, John. *And Our Faces, My Heart, Brief as Photos*. Pantheon, 1984.

Billings, Robert. "Contemporary Influences on the Poetry of Mary di Michele." *Contrasts: Comparative Essays on Italian-Canadian Writing*, edited by Joseph Pivato. Guernica, 1985, pp. 121-152.

Crummey, Michael. "On Winning Inaugural Bronwen Wallace Award." *YouTube*, uploaded by *Writers Trust of Canada*, 28 July 2014, www.youtube.com/watch?v=MFw1NeOzy5U.

di Michele, Mary. Editor. *Anything is Possible: A Selection of Eleven Women Poets*. Mosaic, 1984.

Dubois, René-Daniel. "Magnifique Découverte: An Interview with René-Daniel Dubois" by Josée Lapointe. *la Presse* 26 March 2017. www.lapresse.ca/artslivres/201703/27/01-5082682-bronwen-wallace-magnifique-decouverte.php.

García Márquez, Gabriel and Plinio Apuleyo Mendoza. *The Fragrance of Guava*. Translated by Ann Wright. Verso, 1983.

Helwig, David. *The Names of Things: A Memoir*. Porcupine's Quill, 2006.

Lahey, Anita. "Poetic Justice." *Walrus*. vol. 17, no. 4, 2020, pp. 61-65.

Lee, Dennis. "A Geography of Stories." *Open Letter*, vol 7, no. 9, 1991, pp. 11-14.

Martin, Shelley. "Feminism, Motherhood, and Possibilities in the Writing of Bronwen Wallace." *Feminist Mothering*. State U of New York P, 2008, pp. 61-72.

Meyer, Bruce and Brian O'Riordan. "The Telling of Stories: An Interview with Bronwen Wallace." *Lives & Works: Interviews by Bruce Meyer and Brian O'Riordan*. Black Moss, 1992, pp.100-107.

Miron, Isabelle. *Lieu des origines: poèmes choisis, traduits et présentés par Isabelle Miron avec la collaboration d'Éric Bergeron*. Noroît, 2016.

Smart, Carolyn. *Collected Poems of Bronwen Wallace*. McGill Queen's UP, 2020.

---. "October." *The Way to Come Home*. canpoetry.library.utoronto.ca/smart/poem6.htm

Tregebov, Rhea. *Sudden Miracles: Eight Women Poets*. Second Story, 1991.

Woolf, Virginia. *A Room of One's Own*. 1929. Granada 1981.

Yeats, W.B. "The Symbolism of Poetry." *Essays*. Macmillan, 1924, pp. 188-202.

Wanda Campbell
"Another Country Heard From": A Biography

Bronwen Wallace was born on 26 May 1945 in Kingston, Ontario of United Empire Loyalist stock to Marguerite (Wagar) Wallace known as Peggy, a teacher, and Ferdinand (Ferd) Wallace, a metalworker whose family had lived on the same farm about thirty miles from Kingston for two centuries. Bronwen and her brother Cameron grew up in rural and working-class southern Ontario in a world "where the farmlands draw their nourishment from an ancient mountain range, and houses rise, insistent as the rock and almost as indifferent" (*CM* 22). In "Place of Origin" the poet says, "I keep on living here, without meaning to" (*CM* 11) and other than eight years of her life, Wallace lived in Kingston, citing the light, lake and cost of housing as benefits (*CM* 11), but Kingston continued to be central to her artistic development. "I knew the countryside as well as I knew my own name" (*AW* 164). She died in Kingston on 25 Aug 1989 of cancer of the mouth at the age of 44. But how are we to understand her life beyond these few particulars?

One of the motifs that occurs throughout her oeuvre is that of countries, ranging from "the intricate countries / deep within the eyes" (*CM* 27) in the poem "Common Magic" through "the country of her own damage" (*SPG* 81) in the poem "Bones" to "Another country heard from," the phrase the mother uses as each child speaks in the short story "If This is Love" (*PYT* 60). In an interview Wallace describes how the narrator of *The Stubborn Particulars of Grace* "was on some journey of exploration, through what I find are four countries" (Meyer 104). In addition to the "particulars" of the actual country that she lived in, I suggest we can understand more about her biography by focusing on "four countries" that shaped her life and writing, and the epiphanic moments by which she acquired citizenship in each.

The Country of Politics

> *One of the things I learned from the Sixties, from living in communes, is that what really mattered was not a person's political orientation, but in the end whether they picked up their dirty socks from the middle of the living room floor.* (Wallace qtd. by Meyer 107)

On 24 October 1962, Wallace's Grade 13 History teacher Mr. Ritchie introduced a discussion of the Cuban Missile Crisis by saying, "This may be the last history class we will ever have together" (*AW* 28). Wallace writes: "for the first time in my life it occurred to me that all that stuff in the headlines, and on the radio, and TV had something to do with me, and that in this case it had something to do, directly, with whether I was going to go on living or not" (*AW* 29). Wallace later described that class as "one of the profound revelations" of her life (*AW* 29).

Thus began a lifetime of political awareness and activism that included "an impassioned pro-choice speech from among a group of protestors chained to the visitors' gallery of the House of Commons" (*AW* 8) and the perusal of graveyards for names to give to draft dodgers of the Vietnam War. Wallace was involved in student politics in the Sixties including campaigns for nuclear disarmament and peace, in the Labour movement in the Seventies including left-wing activities of the United Auto Workers Union, and in the Eighties she explored numerous political issues including Free Trade, education, and environmentalism in her "In Other Words" columns in the *Kingston Whig-Standard*. According to di Michele, "Political activity was something that she did when she was very young, and then she started to write" (43), so the two activities continued to inform and enrich each other throughout her life. "As a political person who writes poetry, I know the need for the intimate, inner argument that is the center of a poem" (*AW* 88).

The Country of Poetry

> *Like these stories,*
> *all I have to call a country,*
> *rich as blood, placenta for my future*
> *already seeded in the fields or that woman's face*
> ("Distance from Harrowsmith to Tamworth" *CM* 16)

Wallace graduated from Queen's University with a BA in 1967 and an MA in 1969, but found that her university education "was daily taking [her] further and further away from [her] parents who had worked like hell for [her] to get it" and teaching her "contempt" for her class background and cultural context (*AW* 163-64). Though she had a graduate degree in English literature she had never taken one course in Canadian Poetry or been exposed to more than two or three women writers. She dropped out of the PhD program believing "there was too great a gap between what [she] was studying and what was happening around [her]" (*AW* 163). She proceeded to hitchhike around Canada, working various jobs, and writing "bad T.S. Eliot" (*AW* 203). Then in a Vancouver bookstore in 1970 she came across Al Purdy's *The Cariboo Horses*. In "Lilacs in May: A Tribute to Al Purdy" she describes reading "The Country North of Belleville" and crying "like an idiot" (*AW* 165).

> At that moment, I arrived, in my own country, with land I recognized under my feet, and people I knew around me, and a language I could get my tongue around filling my mouth [...]

His work gave me permission to write about the people I knew, and the landscape I saw, and—most importantly—in the voice I'd heard in my head all my life. (*AW* 165)

Wallace moved back to Ontario and settled in Windsor, described in "Reclaiming the City" not as the *City of Roses* but as "a city of hands" (*CM* 68). There she founded a co-op women's bookstore and became involved in union organizing as well as having a son Jeremy with her partner Ron Baxter in 1974. With encouragement from Phil Hall and Tom Wayman who was then writer in residence at the University of Windsor she began to explore literary citizenship in her "own country" of poetry. In the late 1970s, she returned to Kingston, "no less political, no less committed, but married, with a son, and immensely more relaxed and amused" (Helwig 213). In 1980, Oberon published her first collection of poems *Marrying into the Family* along with Mary di Michele's *Bread and Chocolate*. According to di Michele, this collaboration happened "quite by accident" in that the artwork intended for Wallace's book did not work out, so Oberon paired it with di Michele's poems that were also about family and gender roles.

This marked the beginning of a very productive literary career, where Wallace produced a great deal of fine work in a short time. She also taught creative writing, and mentored many young writers through workshops, teaching creative writing at St. Lawrence College and Queen's University, and serving on the editorial board of *Quarry* magazine. Her work was recognized with the National Magazine Award, the Pat Lowther Award and the Du Maurier Award for Poetry. Her strong narrative tendencies ultimately led her to the form of the short story, an experience she described as "a gift: I was standing in a line-up at Swiss Chalet and a woman started talking to me in my head" (*AW* 210). Throughout her life of creating literature, she was grateful for the opportunity to explore the works of others, "to enter a book as if it were another country and live there with its inhabitants for as long as I wanted" (*AW* 192). Though there were times as a wife and mother she had to "emerge into the country of 'what's for dinner'" (*AW* 199), the country of words was always her true home.

The Country of People

> Some people are a country
> and their deaths displace you.
> ("Coming Through" *CM* 33)

For five years Wallace looked after her good friend Pat Logan who was dying of Hodgkin's disease, an experience related in the "Cancer Poems" that appear in *Signs of the Former Tenant*, and the subject of *All You Have to Do* (1982), one of two documentary films Wallace made in collaboration with her partner Chris Whynot. After her friend's death she knew she wanted to get more involved in the lives of people in need. "I had come to the point, actually, of feeling that I really wanted to get involved in something down to earth and nitty-gritty" (*AW* 22). She began volunteering and then working as a counsellor at Kingston Interval House, a shelter for battered women and their children, for two years, an experience that moved her profoundly, though she was unable to write while doing it, and she was forced to quit after developing a severe allergy to cigarette smoke.

These two difficult experiences deepened and strengthened her work, putting her in touch with people and their suffering in a new way. In May 1987 she launched the column "In Other Words" in the *Kingston Whig-Standard* "in response to a request from the Kingston's women's community that she bring their voice to the pages of the newspaper" (*AW* 6) and in the fall of 1988, she became Writer in Residence at the University of Western Ontario where she learned of the squamous cell carcinoma that would take her life. According to Carolyn Smart, Wallace wrote over and over again in her journal "I have cancer of the mouth" as if "by repeating / [she] might begin to believe it, conquer it, separate it from [her] future" (18), a feat she achieved in that even after her voice was silenced, her words endure.

The Country of Power

I begin, always, with the power of the personal, the private,
the unique in each of us, which resists, survives and can change
the power that our culture has over us. This is what I have learned
from the women's movement and what I try to explore in my poems.
—Bronwen Wallace, "One More Woman Talking"

The final country that grew from and informed all the others was the country of women, and the power of feminism, though it is important to distinguish "power to" from "power over" as Wallace does in "Blueprints for a Larger Life" (*AW* 217). How Wallace arrived here, I will leave to her to express in her own words in a statement she made in 1987 reprinted here with permission from the League of Canadian Poets.

Bronwen Wallace
One More Woman Talking

I can't separate my personal poetics from the life I am leading or from the events that have brought me to this point in it. But since I can't work my whole life history into a statement of poetics, albeit a meandering one, I'll go right straight to one of the high points: a day in May, 21 years ago [1966] , at Queen's University when, with a number of other women, I left a provincial meeting of the Student Union for Peace Action (while the men grumbled that we were being "divisive") to meet and discuss what was then being called The Women's Movement. At the time, I think I probably left the room because it seemed to be Theoretically Correct to do so. I'd been in the peace movement / new left for about three years at this point; I'd started to read Marx; I was big on being T.C. I had absolutely no idea, however, what we would talk about. And I certainly had no idea, theoretically or otherwise, how much this meeting was going to change my life.

What we talked about, in one way or another, for about four hours, was our lives. For me, that meeting represented the first time I had ever been in a room full of women talking *consciously* about their lives, trying to make sense of them, trying to see how the unique and private anecdotes became part of a story that gave each of our lives a public and collective meaning as well.

Since then, the majority of my time has been spent listening to women tell the story of their lives in one form or another. I have attended countless meetings to raise consciousness or disrupt beauty contests or plan anti-nuclear marches; I have joined women chaining themselves to the seats of the House of Commons to protest abortion legislation; I have listened to women tell about being beaten by husbands or boyfriends; I have held a woman's hand while I gave birth and another's as she lay dying. In being part of these events, I share what is common to many women *and* I also experience them uniquely, as myself. Like every other woman, I come to feminism from my own particular pain and strength and am changed by it as no one else will ever be, while at the same time participating in events that change us all. The continuing dialectic between these two elements—the public and the private, the unique and the common—is what I enjoy most about living as I do, in these particular times.

It is also the basis for my poems. I begin with what I have been given: women's stories, women's conversations. Since most of these stories come to me in pretty straightforward, conversational language, that's what I use in the poem, but as I begin to recreate that conversation on the page, I begin to listen to the voice that tells these stories, a voice that is angry sometimes, or frightened, or grieving or ecstatic, and it becomes the voice I have heard in so many women's conversations, a voice that explores *both* the events in the story itself, *and* something else that lies within those events.

This something else is always a mystery for me, since I never know what the poem will discover (just as I never know, in my day-to-day conversations, what any particular woman will discover), but for me, that everyday language is a sort of safety net, a familiar place in which a deeper, often more dangerous exploration can take place. It seems to me that these stories, because they are women's stories, have never been heard before and for that reason, content, *what happens*, is extremely important in itself *and also* in what it conveys about a new way of looking at the world, of being in the world. What I hear in "ordinary conversation" is that movement that goes on among us when we feel safe enough or confident enough or loved enough to explore the power within us, that power which is so often belittled or denied by the society around us (or by ourselves), though it remains the power by which, in our best moments, we manage to survive and to live, sometimes, with grace. That is what I hear in conversation and what I try to record in my poems. If this sounds like a statement of faith, as much as a statement of poetics, that's because it is.

The questions about language which my writing raises, for me at least, have to do primarily with voice, with how to convey this sense of inner discovery at the heart of the most prosaic anecdote. In that sense, my use of everyday language becomes a challenge for me in the poem, as it is in conversation, when we try to convey matters of life-and-death importance with the same words we also use to order a cheeseburger at Harvey's or teach our children how to swim. Sometimes I think the difference is not as great as we like to think, but mostly I just like the challenge.

Another challenge, obviously, lies in the fact that the language I am using has been used in the past primarily to tell men's stories, or, more accurately, to tell everyone's stories from a patriarchal point of view. That point of view is embedded in the language itself and one of the questions raised by this workshop is whether women can speak our piece using it. I definitely experience this problem in my own work, but I have real difficulty with the way the question is posed here and I'd like to take a close look, in particular, at Xavière Gauthier's statement. As you may have guessed, this is now the *Direct Questioning Part of This Paper:*

Women are, in fact, caught in a very real contradiction. Throughout the course of history, they have been mute, and it is doubtless by virtue of this mutism that men have been able to speak and write. As long as women remain silent, they will be outside the historical process. But, if they bend to speak and write as men do, they will enter history subdued and alienated; it is a history that, logically speaking, their speech should disrupt. [Gauthier 162-163]

One of the things I want to say right off about this quote is that I am discouraged—almost offended—by Gauthier's use of "they" rather than "we" in talking about women. I always feel nervous when someone does this; it seems to privilege a sort of distant stance that implies theory is somehow separate from our lives…

There are some other things that bother me too:

Throughout the course of history, they [women] have been mute…

My problem here is that I just can't see it. I mean, I have no trouble seeing Mr. Historian in his study writing his Official Report of the Battle, say, and I have no trouble seeing how the maid brings in his tea and takes it away without a word. In fact, I happen to know that her sister was raped by soldiers after that battle and that her sweetheart was killed in it; I can tell that Mr. H. doesn't even notice her swollen eyes and shaking hands and I'm darn sure none of this will be part of his Account any more than her gossip with the cook will be. BUT I CANNOT, WILL NOT, BELIEVE THAT SHE WAS MUTE ABOUT IT.

Excluded, yes. Mute? Absolutely not!

For one thing, we have other records than those of Mr. H.: diaries, journals, letters, recipes, the liturgy of the Craft, lace, home-remedies, quilts, poems, essays and novels, all of which feminist (and other) historians use all the time to develop other histories than the rather limited Patriarchal Record. Why are we judging women by the same standard that has oppressed us?

As long as women remain silent, they will be outside the historical process.

My Great Aunt Nettie, age 94, is telling me a story. In it her father dies when she is three, leaving her mother alone on a farm with several children. That winter, she discovers she has breast cancer, but since she cannot leave the farm work, she persuades her doctor to come out, chloroform her on the dining room table and remove her breast while her oldest daughter holds the oil lamp. A few days later, she is back in the barn. She goes on living another ten years.

This story, out of all her stories, was the one my great aunt chose to give me at the end of her life. I put it in a poem once. I tell you now. So it becomes History.

But—and this is a Great Big But—regardless of what is recorded, the farm exists, the taxes were paid, the kids raised, the crops planted and harvested. My great grandmother can never be *outside* of these. She exists, she persists, she *moves events* as surely as her cells shape my hands, whether they write about her or no. What are we saying about ourselves, about millions of women like her, when we deny her that? Why are we *starting* from a view of history in which women are *always* the victims?

… if they bend to speak and write as men do, they will enter history subdued and alienated; it is a history that, logically speaking, their speech should disrupt.

On the TV, Margaret Thatcher, a woman who "talks like a man" if I ever heard one. But when I say "talks like a man" I really mean "speaks the language of the Patriarchy" (and by patriarchy I mean a structure, originating in households where the father dominated and reproduced in society, in gender relations, language, ways of seeing, etc.). I'm certainly subdued by and alien to such language. I hear it as the language of power over, of estrangement, of a system which separates men from women, adults from children, people from other animals, people from nature, in a way that expresses difference as opposition, us versus them, life versus death, etc. It is a history which we must disrupt, I believe, both logically and passionately, because our survival as a species depends on it.

I have trouble hearing this in Gauthier's statement, which seems to oppose men, *as a gender*, to women, *as a gender*, without any reference to the relationship between gender and power, say. It leaves me with the impression that anyone who uses the same syntax, vocabulary, etc., as persons of the male gender, are on the side of the devil. Bad guys / good girls. Oppressor / victim. Same old story, just different sides. It's still, as far as I can hear, the patriarchy talking.

One of the questions we are asked, rhetorically, on the Women and Language invitation-to-workshop sheet is "can you imagine a workshop called 'Men and Language?'" It's assumed that we can't, because it's assumed the "men" and "language" are contained in each other. It's assumed that the patriarchy, that patriarchal language, is a monolith and that women are victimized, determined, totally, by the point of view embedded in it.

As far as I can see, such assumptions, unquestioned as they are, create a situation in which *this workshop* becomes a workshop on Men and Language because it poses all the questions in the same old way, uses the same old methods of setting things up.

When I talk of disrupting or changing history, I begin with the assumption that *people* can change, that we are not totally determined by, *bespoken* by, the culture in which we live. I begin, always, with the power of the personal, the private, the unique in each of us, which resists, survives and can change the power that our culture has over us. This is what I have learned from the women's movement and what I try to explore in my poems. I believe that when we speak and write of our lives in this way we also change language, if only because we say things that have never been said before.

A woman who tells someone that her husband is beating her and she wants it to stop. A man who admits that he is violent and asks for help in changing. A poet who writes a poem that challenges conventional syntax and grammar. A feminist reading of *Jane Eyre*. Cyndi Lauper singing "Girls Just Wanna Have Fun." A speech by Helen Caldicott. Two women sitting in a bar talking to each other.

For me, all of these change *language*. They change what can be said about women's lives because they disrupt the silence which has covered so much. They change what we think about each other in a culture which accepts things as they are and constantly erodes our power to change even ourselves. They challenge our assumption that how we speak or see or think is neutral, *not* culturally determined. They permit even feminists to have a sense of humour. They embrace passion and anger and even hysteria as appropriate responses to the present danger of the planet.

I personally believe that language will change—and does change—as women's lives change and not because one way of writing or speaking is theoretically correct. I don't think there is one way of writing and speaking that is theoretically correct. I'm excited by some of the language theory that forms the basis for this workshop. Some of it I just can't understand. Some of it simply doesn't correspond with my own experience, whether of women or of language. That's generally how I respond to most theories.

What matters to me personally is being here, in May, in another room, with another bunch of women, still talking.

[On April 15, 1987, Wallace wrote to Erin Mouré: "I had asked in a previous letter that the poem "Bones" be printed as my "statement" rather than "One More Woman Talking." This is still my wish." (*Two Women Talking* 90)]

Bones

> *for Barb*

A story of yours got this one going,
so I'm sending it back now, changed of course,
just as each person I love
is a relocation, where I take up
a different place in the world.

The way you told it, it was after midnight,
you coming off the late shift, heading home
in a taxi, a woman driving,
and you ask her if she's ever scared
working these hours and she says, "No, I've got this
to protect me!" reaching under her seat

to pull up (you expected a crowbar,
a tire iron) this eight-inch, stainless steel
shank. "The pin from my mother's thigh,"
she tells you, "I got it when they put
one of those new plastic ones in."

Sometimes when I tell myself this story
I get caught up in logistics,
how the doctor must have delivered the thing
from layers of fat and muscle
into one of those shiny dishes
the nurse is always holding
and then she would have,
what? washed it off? wrapped it in towels?
carried it down to the waiting room, the daughter
sitting there, reading magazines, smoking cigarettes?
It's so improbable, like the foetus
pickled in a jar in the science lab in high school,
though other times it's just
there, natural as the light
that bounces off it,
somebody's mother's thigh bone,
for protection, like her face
in the hall light, rescuing you
from a nightmare.

You told me this
during my visit last year
when I'd just quit working
at the crisis centre, that job
that wrenched me round
until each morning stretched, a pale, dry skin,
over the real colour of the day,

ready to spring at me, like the child
whose hand had been held down
on a red-hot burner
reappearing in the face of a woman
met casually at a cocktail party.
Everywhere I went, my work experience
drew me through confessions I couldn't stop,
and I couldn't stop talking about them
so you had to listen
but, being you, in that way that listening
can be active, when the listener re-enters
the country of her own damage
from a new direction.

This can be like watching someone we love
return from the limits a body can be taken to
—a botched suicide, say, or an accident.
Years, it might be, before the eyes or the hands retrieve enough
to offer as a sign,
what doctors think they can detect
on a CAT scan, some pattern in the cells
to show them, once and for all,
how the mind, like the body, makes shape
of what's left, the terrible knowledge
it labours through, slowly regaining itself.

Though on an x-ray, even the bones show up
as light, a translucence that belies their strength
or renders it immeasurable,
like the distances we count on them to carry us,
right to the end of our lives and back again,
and again.

Works Cited

Gauthier, Xavière. "Is There Such a Thing as Women's Writing?" *New French Feminisms*, edited by Elaine Marks and Isabelle de Courtivron, Schocken Books, 1981, pp. 161-64.

di Michele, Mary and Barbara Godard. "'Patterns of Their Own Particular Ceremonies': A Conversation in an Elegiac Mode, between Mary di Michele and Barbara Godard." *Open Letter*, vol 7, no. 9, 1991, pp. 36-59.

Helwig, David. *The Names of Things: A Memoir*. Porcupine's Quill, 2006.

Meyer, Bruce and Brian O'Riordan. "The Telling of Stories: An Interview with Bronwen Wallace." *Lives & Works: Interviews by Bruce Meyer and Brian O'Riordan*. Black Moss, 1992, pp.100-107.

Smart, Carolyn. "The Sound of the Birds" *Common Magic: The Book of the New*. Artful Codger, 2008, pp. 16-23.

Brenda Cantar
Interview With Bronwen Wallace

Arc Interview with Bronwen Wallace at Queen's University, November 2nd, 1987.

ARC: Bronwen, not too long ago you wrote "I like to believe my life / is slowly tidying itself." In your new collection you speak of a "re-mapping of your life." A need for structure in maps or charts seems to figure prominently in your poetry.

WALLACE: I think that the metaphor, maps or charting, is always there. I recognize that I can't separate who I am from the geographical landscape in which I live. In some ways that metaphor arises out of the fact that geography and place are extremely important to me and how I understand my life. I think it also probably has to do with the fact that people's stories or how we tell the stories of our lives, how we chart our way through our life is really important to me. Those two things are really connected for me.

ARC: Is your work autobiographical or is it a fictive sense of events or self that you are creating?

WALLACE: I think I write from my experience. But to write from my experience doesn't necessarily mean that I write from real events in my childhood. I think there may be an emotional truth in the events, at least I hope there is, but the events themselves may be fictional. So it's not directly autobiographical in a narrative sense. But I hope it is in an emotional sense.

ARC: Is any story really autobiographical? It seems to me that as we re-tell our stories of self, of family, the more we re-invent in the telling.

WALLACE: Yes, this is one of the things I'm really interested in, that we're constantly re-inventing our lives. In fact in *Common Magic* I have a poem, "My Son is Learning to Invent Himself." I think we're constantly doing that and that's one of the things that really fascinates me. We get caught up in the idea that a story is about what happens but in fact I think a story is about what happens, yes, but it is also about what we do with what happens or what we make out of what happens which keeps changing as we change.

ARC: Memory shifts and re-locates events all the time we tell the same stories?

WALLACE: Certainly I think there are … well Al Purdy says that every poet only has two or three good poems in them and they just go on revising and I think that's certainly true for me. In some ways you could trace the poem of the family through all four of my books and in some ways it's the same poem. And, in fact, some of the same events re-occur. But that poem keeps changing because I keep changing how I feel about my family or about my relationship to my real, natural family or to my understanding of what the metaphor of the family means.

ARC: Relations and relationships seem central to your work and your own sense of what a family is extends beyond blood ties.

WALLACE: For me I think, the family, in many cases, is one of the most fictional events in my bag of metaphors. My own natural family is not a particularly close one but the metaphor of the family is extremely important for me and not simply the natural family but the family of which we are all a part, the family which connects us. Whether we like it or not we are connected in the same way that our natural family is connected and we can't deny those connections. Or we deny those connections at our peril.

ARC: The poems that have arisen out of your work with battered women at Interval House in Kingston in your new collection, the anger that was a part of an earlier but similar poem, "Dreams of Rescue," seems more controlled in the new ones and I think these poems are far more ominous, perhaps even more frightening because of that control.

WALLACE: That's really interesting. I think when I first began to work at Interval House, when I first began to deal with the whole question of violence against women, I really did have that kind of nice, liberal idea that I was rescuing these people or that I was helping these poor women. And I think that one of the things that I learned from working at Interval House is that there isn't an "us" and "them" situation, that as women we are all in danger and that recognition of that changes not only how I look at the issue but how I look at myself, or how I look at where I am in this society. And it changes what I can do about it.

ARC: What can be done about it and, apart from providing temporary shelter for these women and children, has anything changed in society's attitude towards violence?

WALLACE: Oh I think that things have changed … in terms of the issue of domestic violence, that more and more as a society, we are saying that we will not allow this, we will not hide behind the fact that this is a private family matter and that we will prosecute people who commit this crime. I think that what I was getting at in these poems, though, is that the level at which we accept violence within a family is, for me, connected with the level at which we accept violence in the planet as a whole. We as a culture are accepting more and more violence into our lives.

ARC: Does the fact that we are inured to violence affect the way we, as a society, react to violence against women?

WALLACE: I think it has a lot to do with the way we feel about ourselves as human beings and as women. In some ways, I am talking specifically about violence against women, a particular crime that happens in a particular culture in which misogyny is the ruling world view. But I think that women's experience is also a metaphor for, or is connected to, the experience of powerless people. There is a sense in which most of us, whether we're male or female, are powerless in the threat of the violence that those in power choose to perpetrate. That's the sense of the "Koko" poem, we are all victims of a few things.

ARC: So the past tense of "…The Things I Did Back Then," does not imply that you are not going to do these things again. Was it Auden who said that poems don't change anything?

WALLACE: Was it Auden? Well I don't believe that. The private title for the collection that I had in my mind for *The Stubborn Particulars of Grace* is now the title of the last section "Nearer to Prayers Than Stories" which is a phrase that comes from an essay by John Berger. He's a Marxist critic who wrote *Ways of Seeing*. He has an interesting essay on poetry in which he says that poems, even narrative ones, do not resemble stories. That all stories in one way or another are about battles, about victory and defeat. But, he says, a poem is a way of crying out, a way of saying, this has to be paid attention to *now*. It isn't an appeal to the future, it is an appeal to the *language* to pay attention and in that sense they're nearer to prayers than to stories. Poetry speaks to the immediate and I really believe that and I think in that sense poetry can change things.

I think one of the big myths of our society is that if we are going to change anything we have to continue to be reasonable and I say bullshit to that. Helen Caldicott—the woman who speaks for physicians against nuclear war, in *If You Love This Planet*—she talks about how we must stop being reasonable because we're talking about the death of the planet. There's a place for passion, a place for speaking to the immediate wound and that's where I think poetry can alter things. I hope so.

ARC: Is there not a lack of readers for poetry today, a lack of audience?

WALLACE: On the one hand I think there's a lack of an audience, on the other hand I think that in some ways the audience is changing. I think that the lack of audience comes out of how poetry has been seen or taught. For one thing, poetry, until quite recently, has been a privilege of a particular class and very often a particular gender and a particular world view. To that extent poetry hasn't had much to do with most people's lives. It ends up, because of that, being taught as a problem that you have to solve, that's the way it's taught in High School, poetry is a problem and it is. If you're sixteen, black and female, living in downtown Toronto, Elizabeth Barrett Browning's "How do I love thee" doesn't have a lot of relation to your experience. And certainly Wordsworth's "Daffodils" just doesn't have any but Lillian Allen's poetry might. So I think that there is an audience for poetry that speaks to the experience of that audience. What I really notice is that there are a number of women poets that are becoming really popular like Lorna Crozier as one example, and popular with people who don't read poetry. And I think that's because it's that poetry is not this arcane mystical kind of art form. Another way of looking at it too is that the most popular form of poetry in our part of the century is rock and roll which is, in many ways, an incredibly sophisticated poetic art form. When I do poetry workshops with High School kids I find that they listen to Bob Dylan, John Lennon, David Bowie, the Talking Heads, all of whom are incredibly sophisticated. And then they turn around and say, "we don't understand poetry" but of course they do.

ARC: So you're talking about how we 'label' art. What do we do then, Bronwen, about the 'canon'? What do we do with Wordsworth if he doesn't speak to our particular experience?

WALLACE: I think it does speak to some people's experience obviously. But I think we have to expand the 'canon.' I think it is really sad that many University English departments do not choose to include a great deal of contemporary work. In making that choice they also choose to maintain a certain class and gender bias. It shuts out a large number of people.

ARC: Is that not altering?

WALLACE: I think it's altering but I think it could alter more quickly.

ARC: I was encouraged by the difference in the new edition of the Norton Anthology. The inclusion of many more female writers in the Medieval and Renaissance sections, for instance, Mary Sidney alongside Philip Sidney.

WALLACE: Yeah and I think that's important. The other thing that I see is that there are many ways in which the academic community is no longer the 'cutting edge' of culture and learning that it once was. There are a lot of things that happen at poetry readings, on film and at rock concerts that say a lot more about what we are as a culture than what happens in the university.

ARC: Will that not lead to a further widening of the gap between critic and artist?

WALLACE: That's a hard question. Not necessarily. From my own experience, the most valuable thing I learned from doing a graduate degree in English at Queen's in a very traditional way is that I learned tools that allow me to look at most cultural forms and understand how to read them. I may choose not to question the class bias of that education but if I do choose to question that, the tools that I have I can use. The tools that allow you to read a poem by Wordsworth can also be used to read a song by David Bowie. We are still talking about the language. I think the problem is not the tools but the unquestioned political bias in those tools. It's up to us as individual scholars how we use those tools.

ARC: On the topic of political bias, where does your female sensibility or where does committed feminism become more political than it is literary and does any self-respecting writer want this? This is a question that often arises.

WALLACE: That's a question that doesn't question its own biases because all art is political and if I choose at this point in time to write poems about pine trees or about smiling babies or sunsets, that's a political choice. If I choose to do that in the face of what I see around me I've made a political choice. And I think the fact that I'm seen as a political poet because I write poems about Interval Houses says a great deal about our narrow understanding of what is political. I'm not talking about political as the NDP but as how we live our lives.

ARC: Polly Fleck has said, speaking about women poets, that "women must surface but in the mainstream." I would argue that there is no mainstream for women.

WALLACE: At this point in time I would agree with you. Simply being a woman who speaks out is still a radical act. We live in a culture where we still refer to women doctors and women lawyers, when Sheila Copps has a baby it's front page news. It seems to me that even in the most traditional places it's still an act of rebellion to simply be there as a female. So I think you're right, there is no mainstream unless you become someone like Margaret Thatcher although even the criticism that is heaped on her has a gender component.

ARC: How does a gender component become eradicated? If women write of women's concerns which are often domestic, does that not compound the gender bias, is there not a risk involved?

WALLACE: I think the risk involved is allowing ourselves to think that women's experience, domestic poems, have nothing to do with what we like to call 'universal human experience'. Because it means that we've never questioned what we know about 'universal human experience'. It's a truism now but it's still one we have trouble with that what we understand of 'universal human experience' has generally been male. And that goes for everything from how doctors understand the human body to the fact that we think that poems about having a baby or a Jane Austen novel are less universal than *War and Peace*. Yet 50% of the human race has the opportunity to give birth to the future. Those are both 'universal human experiences', we've just never included both. To get through that gender bias we have to see that everything is gendered, there are all of our separate experiences which make up what we are as human beings.

ARC: How we are made up as human beings is through the language we speak. Language creates us and if there is this male bias in language how do we break through that?

WALLACE: That's where there's a really large wide-ranging debate as you probably know with women writers. There is lots of language centred writing which I think is really exciting, I'm thinking of Gail Scott or Erin Mouré or Daphne Marlatt. I think that stuff is really necessary and interesting. For me, I know that I just can't do that any more than I'm any good on a skateboard. What I see my talent in is taking what is ostensibly a standard narrative form and by giving it a female voice. I think I also change the shape and direction of that narrative. That's what I'm doing although I recognize that I'm not doing the kind of radical experimental things with language that someone like Erin Mouré is doing.

ARC: Penny Kemp also plays with language very seriously, exposing and dismantling its seemingly opaque nature.

WALLACE: I think we need all those things. It's not only women who are doing this. People like Stephen Scobie, Rudy Wiebe and Robert Kroetsch and all those post-modernists. What concerns me in the discussion about language among women writers is when it stops being one option and starts being 'the way to write' or you're not a feminist if you don't write a language-centred poem. It becomes prescriptive. Then it sounds to me like a kind of Stalinism of the feminist movement which I have no patience for. Being a hardcore anarchist, I have no patience with that.

ARC: I have difficulty defining the feminist movement in some kind of totalizing sense.

WALLACE: Yeah, it's everywhere, the FBI is right, subversion is everywhere. I get impatient with people who say if you don't do such and such you're not a feminist.

ARC: Do you not get equally impatient with the denial of feminism? I often hear women writers deny that they are feminists.

WALLACE: Like in "I'm only a writer"? That's the same kind of denial as denying that all art is political. It's denying your specificity as a human being and I can't see the point in doing that. I don't think that as human beings we can do anything but write from our own experience of the world. Being female is part of the experience as is being black or white, working class or middle class, gay or straight or whatever. All of that affects how we see the world and how we write. The question we never ask ourselves is why we see what we are as a limitation. To me what I am is not a limitation but an infinite possibility. We're really screwed up in this idea that we have to transcend some barrier to get to the universal. We are the universal, all of us.

ARC: Writers, male or female, face similar professional concerns. What does being a woman add to those professional concerns?

WALLACE: What has happened in the past, and this is really changing, is that inclusion in anthologies, acceptance for publication and reviews have depended on an unspoken standard about what human experience is, that women don't fit. So their work is seen as too personal or too private. There was this wonderful review of Mary di Michele's second book in which she was reviewed with two male writers. The reviewer ended up by saying that she was technically the most interesting but that since she wrote only as a woman she was limited. That kind of thing has really held women back. Our reading is always gendered and if we're reading a text without questioning that gender bias then sure there's going to be fewer women in anthologies, fewer women published, fewer women who are members of the League of Canadian Poets, etc.

ARC: What is the solution? Women review women?

WALLACE: No. I think there are a number of solutions. Part of the solution is continuing to draw attention to it at the Writer's Union, the League. Various people have spoken to the review editors and talked about gender bias. The more that issue gets raised the more people have to question people who have the power to make those decisions. I also think that people, men and women are changing. There are lots of really positive reviews of women's work by men.

ARC: You don't think it's because it's the fashion or 'au courant'?

WALLACE: I don't really care.

ARC: We have spoken about the power of language. When you write do you find yourself questioning what you write?

WALLACE: Constantly. I revise a lot. Endlessly. Working on the manuscript of *The Stubborn Particulars of Grace*, for the first time I had an editor who went over that manuscript line by line, poem by poem. So that I felt that I was really challenged to my limit and that was really valuable. Donna Bennett was a really valuable guide.

ARC: That sense of sharing seems important in all your poems. But there's also an overwhelming sense of loss, of friends, of time, losses that you feel compelled to keep going over.

WALLACE: Yeah and I think that's the other side of the theme of the family, the connectedness, the theme of how stubborn our particulars are, the fact that we are also completely alone in the face of our own mortality, in the face of the choices we make. So we are both completely alone and deeply and inextricably connected.

ARC: What, who, are your literary connections? Women haven't had a 'tradition' to work in. Are women creating their own myth structures?

WALLACE: Oh yeah. What we were saying earlier about reviews is that we do have to create our own tradition in a sense. A tradition that gives us permission to talk and write about the things we write about. There's this wonderful interview with an American poet, Philip Levine, in which he says he doesn't understand how Keats could watch his brother die from tuberculosis and the guy gets two lines. And he says if America took my brother and killed him at seventeen, I would never get over it. I don't think Keats ever got over it but he couldn't write about it because he didn't have the tradition I have. And I think that's really true from women until very recently. I think that I can write about what I write about because of Margaret Atwood, Dorothy Livesay, P.K. Page, Elizabeth Brewster who have given me permission to do that. Given me language, images and metaphors.

ARC: Are those writers your chief influences?

WALLACE: Well yes, but in terms of my new book, one of the major influences on how those poems work is Galway Kinnell, and what I learned from him in how to structure the line. I also owe a debt to Al Purdy. His structures really gave me permission to structure my poems in the form of a narrative when every other woman I know is writing lyrics. In terms of vision I am certainly influenced by Alice Munro and definitely Flannery O'Connor.

ARC: Do you feel, as a woman poet, you have to deconstruct patriarchal myths in order to reveal some of the distorted figurations of women?

WALLACE: I feel that if I write a good, honest poem and do the best job I can, I'm doing that in terms of being honest about my experience as a woman in this particular place and time. That does deconstruct patriarchal myths about women and humanity, society and all kinds of things. I don't think I can consciously do that as language-centered poets do.

ARC: But you do it unconsciously?

WALLACE: If I can go by the anger my work engenders in some critics and the positive reception my work gets from a lot of women, I must be doing that.

ARC: Have you engendered anger from critics?

WALLACE: Oh yeah. In a review, I think it was the *Ottawa Citizen* for *Common Magic*, the reviewer said, "men get short shrift in feminist poems." I don't know whether the word shrill was used but it was there by implication right? And the reviewer was extremely concerned that there were no men in the poems unless they were old or children which a) isn't true and b) so what. There have been reviews where it's said that I used the "you" as though it were universal and that I'm only talking about myself. Who's Wordsworth talking about?

ARC: How do you feel then about having Women's Studies departments? Do they not lead to increasing ghettoization of women?

WALLACE: I think we're in a ghetto anyway. We might as well have affirmative action, clean up the neighbourhood. The university is a male studies department so I think to openly affirm that we are going to have a women's studies department at least calls attention to the fact and allows a place or it becomes a means for turning out good feminist scholars. At some point universities will become truly Human Studies departments and then perhaps women's studies can disperse. I think there has to be a place in the University where women learn their history and since it's not going to happen in a regular history class, and I don't see that happening, then women have to do that for themselves.

ARC: Where does the artist fit into changing society, the world?

WALLACE: I can't answer for other artists but my answer would be the same as García Márquez: "I do that by writing as well as I can."

Mary di Michele
The Stubborn Silence

The very stone one kicks with one's boot will outlast Shakespeare.
—Virginia Woolf, *To the Lighthouse*

I think Bronwen would have liked my use of a quotation from Woolf to frame this memoir essay about her and her writing, and yet it's with some difficulty I return to writing about Bronwen, with some resistance to resurrecting those feelings of grief and anger. All I can offer is this rambling meditation on poetry, mortality, and memory. The last time I saw Bronwen was in the summer of 1989, when I made the trip to Kingston from Toronto to visit her, to say goodbye. I was leaving for Italy. She was gravely ill, and maybe I was still "in denial;" I promised to visit again when I returned in September. Her last words to me were: "Or I'll come to see you." What was the expression on her face? (I wish I could call it back up in my mind with the precision I remember her words.) Was it a bit bemused? Or ironic in a way that doesn't preclude sympathy. I remember feeling relieved when she said that. I think that she was absolving me from the guilt of leaving, of being healthy, of being alive.

To write this essay I turned to her writing, more reliable than my memory, rereading the poems and stories, not as a critic might, but as a friend picking up old letters and photographs to see her face again, and to hear that voice that will no longer speak with breath. In his poem "Byzantium," W.B. Yeats called it "death-in-life and life-in-death" the "superhuman" voice that speaks to us through "A mouth that has no moisture and no breath," (*Collected Poems* 280) through art, through the poem.

I have written about her in poetry, "Angel of Slapstick," and in the paper "Snowsuits and Headbands," for the *Common Magic* conference held at Queen's University in Kingston in 2008, on the twentieth anniversary of her death. Twenty years have become thirty years.

There can be no new words from Bronwen Wallace, we will never hear her speak again. There is only silence coming from the other side of the river Styx, a silence Bronwen might have called *stubborn*.

> She's been dead for a long time now.
> You'd thought that would make a difference,
> but it hasn't.
> ("Coming Through" *CM* 32)

The 'she' in the lines above refers to Bronwen's friend, Pat Logan. "Coming Through" is a poem in Bronwen's second full collection, *Common Magic*, published in 1985, while "The Cancer Poems" that narrate and meditate on Pat's death from Hodgkin's disease are included in her first full collection, *Signs of the Former Tenant*. That book was published in 1983, a mere two years before. Time always makes a difference, and more than that, it makes differences. We, those still living, continue to change; she does not except barely perceptibly, in our unreliable and morphing memories.

Those Cancer poems were written in the third person, a voice extremely rare in Bronwen's poetry. In the poem, "Fourth Dream" of the sequence, the dying Pat is transformed into an art object like the "Miracle, bird or golden handiwork" immortalized in Yeats' "Byzantium" (*Collected Poems* 280). I think of the old man in this poem as Yeats himself; together they are transfigured:

> … and she turns to
> his face blazing
> and the tree above their heads
> all sudden crystal

shines with leaves and fruit
flashing like prisms
birds of blown glass
sing and
radiant as the tree
she spins all night
in the brilliant shapes
of their song
("Fourth Dream" *SFT* 96)

In the last of the Cancer poems, "A Stubborn Grace," Bronwen returns to using her own voice, and contemplates what she has learned about death from Pat:

I always thought death
was something you came up
against and entered
with deliberate ceremonies   formal words
but here where you are my own dying
enters me
like the song a friend might sing
in the last moments of a party
…
until the last notes drop
into the still pools
the song has made in each of us
(*SFT* 106)

It is hard to read these lines without some sense of cosmic irony: "but here where you are my own dying / enters me" (*SFT* 106). Art is that song we sing together, it is choral.

Some people are a country
and their deaths displace you.
Everything you shared with them
reminds you of it: part of you in exile
for the rest of your life.
("Coming Through" *CM* 33)

It seems a kind of inversion to feel the living self as the one exiled. The beloved friend was a place the poet could not return to. Beyond borders, beyond language; that exile is a kind of punishment for continuing to live. There's guilt there too, the kind of guilt that Bronwen understood and that I think she wanted to relieve me of the last time I saw her:

in these last few weeks your hands
grew whiter than snow on your windowsill
and beside them mine
even in their pasty winter paleness
blushed   I was almost ashamed to touch you
I was so alive
("A Stubborn Grace" *SFT* 109)

"Dying made everything possible" ("Sorceress" *SFT* 97). How to understand this opening line, turning it over and over in my mind, recalling a favourite quotation Bronwen often cited from Flannery O'Connor, and that she used as an epigraph for *The Stubborn Particulars of Grace*: "Possibility and limitation mean about the same thing." In the limitation that is our mortality, possibility may lie in the sense of the transformative power of death, the lifting out of the body, the self, and into the formal, the public, into the poem:

> and daily she learned
> the source of her magic
> saw in the mirror how
> she grew more beautiful
> grew vast and complex
> became the city
> she inhabited
> ("Sorceress" *SFT* 98)

Death as the limitation on life is also what enables the dying Pat to see even the light as new: "she saw for the first time / exactly how the light lay / on the kitchen table" ("Sorceress" *SFT* 98). I see the powers recognized in "Sorceress" linked to the theme embodied in the title, *Common Magic*. Bronwen makes a big leap in her writing in this book. For her death opened up the chasms in what we call reality; a domestic city night scene is suddenly seen as otherworldly:

> Nothing is solid now. Against the sky the trees
> are so still they vibrate with the effort
> of holding themselves in and the walls of the houses
> hesitate as they might dissolve,
> revealing the lives behind them, intricate
> and enchanted as the lives of dolls.
> ("Coming Through" *CM* 30)

The change in Bronwen's style here is not in subject matter, but in apperception, death as duende transforms the seeing in these poems. It entered her; it entered the poetry. But not to embrace "the artifice of eternity" (Yeats, "Sailing to Byzantium" *Collected Poems* 218) rather to challenge that trope with that of story as passed on through generations by living voices: "As the cadence of an old woman's voice / becomes the line that will lead others / into the territory her people saw" ("Testimonies" *SPG* 47). Art itself is not life; this seems to me the beginning of her rejection of the golden bird trope. While the art object in Yeats' Byzantium poems is the golden bird, avatar for the poet and their poem, Bronwen seems to mock it:

> … the parrot up in Carcross, N.W.T.,
> a bird someone brought over the pass
> during the gold-rush and left at the Caribou Hotel
> where it lived for another sixty years
> entertaining customers by singing
> nineteenth-century bar-room ballads
> in a cockney accent. The voice of a dead miner
> kept on in a brain the size of an acorn
> ("Testimonies" *SPG* 47)

The poem is brought down many registers from the Olympian realm; it's no golden bird, it's a Yukon parrot talking in a bar. In the fairy tale, the golden bird turns out to be a poor substitute for the living nightingale. And for Bronwen art is a poor substitute for the beloved friend. In her story, "The Scuba Diver in Repose" (*PYT* 165-186) the protagonist photographer burns her photos of her now dead lover. They, her art, could not replace the living man. And yet the photographs charged her with remembering, remembering when she wanted to forget.

The poet's voice—I remember Bronwen telling me how disappointed she was when she heard Galway Kinnell, a poet she admired, read at Queen's. She described his as a radio voice; she said that he broadcast rather than spoke to the audience. Bronwen speaks directly and intimately through her writing. I still hear her voice in the poems, and I also hear it in the narrator's voice in her short stories. What is the poet's voice that we recognize in a poem? Is it merely style? Word choice, subject matter, and tone, or that hardest to delineate, that amorphous aspect of voice? No, that voice was embodied; there is a gender to sound, there is even sexual preference. And so I hear an echo of that body in her text. It can't say anything new, or different from what was written; it's a parrot (not to be underestimated as a bird) and readers may hear it differently over the years. So it evolves and continues to live. Poetry is immortal if the stone that's kicked is a fossil that recalls the contours of the living creature; Bronwen Wallace will be immortal, as in remembered, as long as we read her, as long as we're human, and perhaps even beyond that.

Angel of Slapstick

for Bronwen Wallace

> Light from the dust
> of a drawer.

The beetles don't fly out when Dewdney opens his desk. No, they show off their brilliance without stirring. The shining is concentrated in their shells as if from a trace of what originally moved them. Their legs have lost all urgency. Curled and withered, they are blacker than in life. As if the light has drained entirely into the armoured back. The backs are green. They are glinting. All gold is fool's gold. What is most precious are these once-living emeralds, which have inched their way, which have known light as if it were a form of intention. The construction of their wings splits the crystal of the back.

When short people sit down to drink tea, their feet tread air. They exercise their ankles because their soles feel vulnerable.

"Evolution is on your side," Dewdney reassured me.

    (But not the design
    of the furniture.)

Descended perhaps from something that crawled out of the skin
of one of the smaller meat-eating dinosaurs, from a relative of
tyrannosaurs, its crazy locomotion between flying and walking.

    We have forgotten more than we know
    about earth.

           *

    Flying with you to the West Coast
    I tried to explain how my balance
    was a special gift, an adaptation,
    the smaller body a truce
    between the oversized head and the planet.

    It's fall 1981 and we are seated in the Air
    Canada jet by the wing.
    Because you are ten inches taller you can more
    easily command, from the stewardess, drinks.
    You are ten inches taller yet we have the same size
    feet. "A deformity," you say. And it's good to be
    with you, Bron. That your walk is a form of ballet.
    That your height is stature which cannot be measured.

All the things you have taught me and our place in the story I can't get
in one poem I can't mend even the simplest break with
this improvised sling
                over the abyss.
    When I recall your face.

Slowly. So that my life with you is replayed.
And I watch it like a film. In the dark
my eyes fill, images dissolve
bodies spill into one another and become one body
when it's erotic and not a mass
grave.

Rumi wrote that we are all like unmarked
boxes shifting from one thing
into another. Maybe we are like frames
in a film we can't just look
at the negatives.
The print. We have to run
the whole thing. Live
faster than we can be stilled.

Where else would I find how to make soup
and how to make poems on the same page?
At home with you, it is written
in the same language. So when the raisin from a curry
floats up in my fish chowder I think of you
the poet who understood *metaphor*
is still the Greek word for *porter*
and as Berger reminds us, the service better
rendered is not comparison, but transportation.
Our baggage. Our ghosts.
Not for simile, but for discovery

"of those correspondences of which the sum would be proof of
the indivisible totality of existence."

Listen. What we can become together
without even thinking about it.

In spite of its small betrayals,
trusting the body.

Because I was thinking
of you, the way your magic
is in the domestic,
no tricks, just practical technique,
as simple as cracking eggs in half
with the slightest flick
of the wrists so that no little bits
of shell spoil the easyover or scrambled,
and at the same time I was looking up
for street signs, myopically
making my way out of *Badlands*
I had been reading on the subway
and I know I should have been
more fully there
for breathing until breath is
wind turned outside in
blowing through us cleanly
as those few ashes
spilling out of Carolyn's
purse. It's you. That ash not you.
You are Orpheus

scattered among your friends. Many.
You are many. Now even with the best
acoustics in the world, without wood,
without the body
of the violin,
where is music?
The bow saws to the applause

of one hand. Harmonious instrument.
When all we who miss you want is what was
heard off-key. The woman.

So because I was more with you than on Bloor sidewalks,
I was surprised when I looked down
and my feet were drawn into quicksand
from the Badlands. Even a little
reading can be a dangerous thing.

What really happened is that I had walked several feet without

sinking
into cement. Jumping out of my shoes as if my ankles knew
wings. And the man with the white
hat from Public Works said: "How in hell
did you do that, lady!"
And you can have faith in this
Bron, in Public Works and the *common courtesies*.
He helped me. He found a pole to pull out my shoes,
Cleaned them off and drove me to my job.
And I was on time.

So I think of my way of bumbling along on earth like those bees
which circumvent gravity and all we know of the laws of
aerodynamics to fly, I think of that little feat as a story I want
you to interpret. Stretching, by the ligaments of language

not flight, the miracle is
not our altitude on the DC-7,
nor the birds in which we glimpse
from their fierce appetite, our familiars.
The first dinosaurs moving among us.

No, the miracle is not
in flight, but
in the bones of what may be
in time
whether winged or grounded,
whether ostrich or woman

I might have continued
to look for redemption
by cement, for baptism,
in gravel, sand, and water,
if not for you. And the angel
of slapstick. And look
my feet take me without my head.
How near.
                    How far.

This gentleness we learn
from what we can't heal.
—Bronwen Wallace

Susan Rudy
"A reach for what we only hope is there": Bronwen Wallace's Writing at the Interval

It's been over thirty years since I met Bronwen Wallace in 1989. Our mutual friend and my colleague Eric Savoy had suggested we invite her to do a reading at the University of Calgary while she was in Alberta in February of that year. We did, and she read, and we hosted a lovely dinner for her. She died six months later. Our uncanny experience of making angels in the snow with her on our way home from that gathering is described in our Introduction to *Particular Arguments*, the issue of *Open Letter* in which the essay below first appeared.

This sad anniversary brings happier news, as Carolyn Smart's edition of the *Collected Poems of Bronwen Wallace* (McGill-Queen's 2020) which includes all of Wallace's published poems and a selection of previously unpublished early work, and Campbell's edition of essays on Wallace's work (Guernica 2022) will bring renewed attention to this feminist writer and activist whose considerable body of work has still not received the academic or indeed public attention it deserves. As Erin Mouré wrote in response to Smart's announcement of the publication of the *Collected Poems*, "This is a momentous event ... for decades Bronwen Wallace's poems have been very difficult to access, yet they should still be part of the conversation of poetry, politics, subjectivities, lives, feminism, forms" (*Facebook*, 10 Jan. 2020. Cf. Mouré, *Two Women Talking*).

My 1991 article reprinted below was published under Susan Rudy Dorscht, the name I assumed between 1983, when I got married, until the mid 1990s when my emerging feminist consciousness gave me a way to understand that I needn't have added the name of the person to whom I was married to my name. The issue of how women are known, and what record we leave—either in terms of publications or progeny—remains of crucial importance. In this article I suggested that Wallace's is a "Writing at the Interval" which "opens up the gaps between the given world of patriarchal ideology and the world that a feminist perspective sees and makes possible" (Rudy Dorscht and Savoy, "Introduction" 8).

In guest-editing the special issue of *Open Letter* on Wallace's work in 1991, Eric Savoy and I were astonished at the dearth of academic attention to her work even then. At the time, I was more of a poststructuralist than a feminist, but I was participating in (and often found myself crying during or after) a weekly feminist theory reading group with Susan Bennett, Tracy Davis, and Jeanne Perreault, all of whom went on to become eminent scholars. A quick glance through a few of Wallace's books made me realise I wanted to write about the work of this woman who had chosen titles like "A Simple Poem for Virginia Woolf" (*SFT* 48-51), "Getting the Words for It" (*SFT* 17-19), and "The Woman in This Poem" (*SFT* 79-82). I could see that Wallace had written about many of the issues I was struggling with in my own life, including what to do about an emerging awareness that I was a lesbian in a world that hadn't accommodated my existence. Rereading my 1991 essay in 2020, I can see that I was looking in Wallace's work for a way to understand why the woman I felt myself to be—that is, a lesbian—seemed both impossible and increasingly desirable.

When I met Bronwen Wallace in February 1989, I was 28, an assistant professor at the University of Calgary, married to a kind man, mother of a young daughter, straight (apparently). A month later, I would be pregnant with my second daughter. I couldn't imagine giving all of that up for an alternative that seemed impossible. As I wrote of Wallace's poem "The Maiden Aunts", from *Marrying Into the Family*, something in the faces of unmarried women seems "incongruous"– the signifier doesn't correspond to the expected signified—"like the photograph / that catches its subject unaware / startles into being / an attitude so unexpected / that the most familiar relative stares for a moment / before she tosses the thing aside turns / impatiently to poems more appropriate / for gilt-edged albums" ("Writing at the Interval" 87 *infra*).

Though "the modern [i.e. 1980s!] style" of the so-called "maiden aunt" [i.e. lesbian] is "robust well-tailored", and they "hold important positions in offices hospitals" (*MF* 55), the maiden aunts were not, as far as I knew then, mothers. They were "the thing" tossed aside:

> They are the ones who in Victorian novels
> fade into the pages
> with a discreet hint of lavender
> [...]
> something about them requires still
> a certain delicacy
> shadowy tales of jiltings   grand renunciations
> in the name of religion or family loyalty
> (*MF* 55)

Yet in Wallace's attempt to "startle into being" the image of women as "renegade flowers" opening "to the dark" (*MF* 56), I still argued, and felt, that the closing image of the poem offered "an empowering, radicalizing, and sensuous place for women": an image of a woman opening herself completely to the mind and body of another woman. Speaking of Wallace's poem "Intervals," I argued that Wallace

> challenges the ideology of what the poem calls "love's body / where the prince and the princess live / happily ever after. / Your own childhood" ("Intervals" 59). The poem itself is an

interval that opens up the possibility of meaning for women by rereading "what we have been given."
("Writing at the Interval" 80 *infra*)

The work of Bronwen Wallace gave and gives me, and all her readers, ways to reread, challenge, and look for alternatives to the heterosexual and other scripts that we have been given. As I wrote then, these poems are written "to get to you" (Wallace, *CM* 56), to "disturb and move you" ("Writing at the Interval"). They exist, still, as "a reach / for what we only hope / is there" ("Anniversary" *SPG* 55).

I am writing this introduction in January 2020. I am 58, based in London (England), living with—indeed married to—my lesbian partner. I am also a mother and grandmother. My current research focusses on what it means to be a woman now. As I argue elsewhere, queer women—especially cis and trans lesbians—have more in common than contemporary fissures either allow for or acknowledge (Rudy, "Gender's Ontoformativity"). Indeed, lesbians like myself, who recognised our queer sexuality in the 1970s and 1980s, have in common with trans women the shared condition of having been, in the words of the 1970s radical feminist Marilyn Frye, "spat summarily out of reality" (173). We also share the experience of refusing to accept this condition. To make this argument, I draw on sociologist Raewyn Connell's concept of gender ontoformativity (*Gender and Power* 211). "The human body itself," Connell wrote, "is an object of practice" (*Gender and Power* 78). If the person is "constructed as a 'project' of realizing oneself in a particular way," that project is "onto-formative," constitutive of social reality (Connell, "Transsexual Women and Feminist Thought" 210). Moreover, "the results of practice do not sit around outside time, but themselves become the grounds of new practice" (Connell, *Gender and Power* 79). Gender is ontoformative in that we are both in it and able to shape it otherwise.

Although she wouldn't have used the term, Bronwen Wallace began to teach me about gender's ontoformativity. In her interview with Janice Williamson, given during her visit to Alberta in February 1989, included in our special issue of *Open Letter*, and later published in *Arguments with the World*, Wallace said that "If we are going to live with wholeness or integrity in the world, we have to pay attention to the particulars and politics of where we are" (*AW* 205). I have written this introduction to situate the "particulars and politics" of where I was in 1989 and to articulate where I am now on these issues, but I am happy to reproduce 'Writing at the Interval' (1991) below as a testament, not only to why Wallace's poetry still matters, but also to the difference that poetry can make in the lives of its readers.

Writing at the Interval

1. Getting the Words for It[1]

> There are maps of it and lights to show us
> when to walk, where to turn.
> What I want you to know is that it isn't enough.
> (Wallace "To Get To You" *CM* 56)

> Nothing is ever the same as they say it was.
> It's what I've never seen before that I recognize.
> (Arbus epigraph *SFT* 5)

> I write from what I am given.
> (Wallace "Why I Don't (Always) Write Short Stories" *AW* 178)

In *Female Desire: Women's Sexuality Today*, Rosalind Coward analyses the cultural practices—magazine ads, advice columns, popular romances—which construct women's pleasure, "the way our desire is courted even in our most everyday experiences as women" (16), and comes to the following significant conclusion: "[g]ood girls enjoy what they're given but what they're given may not always be good for them" (14). If we understand the shifting meaning of the word "good" in this sentence, we know, somehow, that current ideology is not good for us; Wallace's theory of writing—"I write from what I am given"—speaks of this way of being. We do not simply have to "enjoy" what we are given; we can say that we don't enjoy it; we can challenge it; we can write about it.

In quite particular ways, Wallace's poems are written out of what she has been "given": "[n]ot just images, words, sounds, voices. But a particular life, as a woman, in a particular family and community, at this time in history" (*AW* 178). As the anonymous information on the cover of *The Stubborn Particulars of Grace* says, "Wallace speaks to us, in a voice that we immediately recognize as close to our own…. She awakens us to our own reality." Jeanette Lynes, in a review of the same book, speaks of the orderliness of the details in Wallace's poems: "junk piled in a garage, photographs, the difficulty and sometimes the boredom of working at a shelter for battered women, traumatic beginnings and endings, Sunday dinners, birthdays, anniversaries, and most significantly, perhaps, *stories*" (213). When we read Wallace, we read ourselves and our stories.

Or do we? For Louis Althusser, it is an ideology that we "live, move, and have our being:"

It is indeed a peculiarity of ideology that it imposes (without appearing to do so, since these are "obviousnesses") obviousnesses as obviousnesses, which we cannot fail to recognize and before which we have the inevitable and natural reaction of crying out…. "That's obvious! That's right! That's true!" (171)

Although I recognize much of what Wallace was given and gives me—I too am a white woman born into a middle-class Ontario family in the second half of the twentieth-century; I too became a daughter, wife, mother. And everywhere there were, as Wallace's poem "To Get To You" says, "maps of it and lights to show us / when to walk, where to turn" (*CM* 56); —I proceed cautiously when my reaction is so unequivocally "that's obvious, that's right, that's true." And so do Wallace's poems. "It's never easy," she writes, "[e]ven the effort of a few steps / from the bedroom to the kitchen … / All I know is that it's learned / by doing, over and over again / … until you don't need to think about it" (*CM* 55). Wallace's poems are constructed to make us think about it.

While many readers note the verisimilitude of Wallace's work, to notice only that is to ignore the self-consciousness and anxiety about the "obviousness" of things which the poems articulate. Phrases like "how else to say it" ("Thinking with the Heart" *CM* 59), "You'd never use that word, of course" ("Blackflies" *CM* 72), or "There's only so much anyone can say" ("Splitting it Up" *CM* 66) all of which are first lines of poems, articulate the limitations our ways of saying impose on our "ways of seeing," to use John Berger's phrase.[2] Moreover, these poems make us connect the way we see with what we know and point out the ideological assumptions that both limit and make possible what we can know.[3] Ideology is "what we are given." A critique of ideology is what Wallace's poems give us.

The critique of ideology begins by locating gaps in what we are given, what the narrator in "Between Words," repeating the words of the woman in the poem whose story she is retelling (itself a writing strategy that encourages us to read what we are given), calls "the stubborn silences / that grow / between the words" (*SFT* 61), what I call, drawing on "Intervals," from *The Stubborn Particulars of Grace*, the interval. "Intervals" struggles to articulate the experiences of women living and working at a particular interval—

Interval House, a crisis centre for battered women in Kingston, Ontario. The poem is also highly self-conscious about the meaning it attempts to construct and includes an extended consideration of the word "interval" scattered at intervals throughout the second part of the poem and entitled, ironically, "Free Speech." The following is a condensation of the etymology of the word "interval" in the poem. Notice how the dictionary definitions are juxtaposed with information about the House itself:

> *Interval House.*
> *Interval: originally*
> *from the Latin* inter vallum,
> *the space between ramparts,*
> *walls, between two events,*
> *two parts of an action, a period*
> *of cessation, a pause*
> …
> *A house that can accommodate*
> *20 according to regulations,*
> *30 in a pinch, since we don't*
> *turn anyone away, 32*
> *if we use the old couch*
> *in the back office, maybe 35*
> *if most of them are children*
> *which they are*
> …
> *Between any fits or periods of disease*
> *an open space lying*
> *between two things*
> *or two periods of one thing*
> …
> *The distance between persons*
> *in respect of position, beliefs, etc.*

> *or between things in respect of their qualities,*
> *the difference of pitch between two*
> *musical sounds, an opening*
>
> *a gap*
>
> *a 24-hour crisis line*
> (Wallace "Intervals" *SPG* 61-63)

As the attention to the meanings of Interval House make it possible for us to see, the words *Interval* and *House*, when spoken together, open up a gap, a contradiction, in patriarchal ideology. Interval House is a place that is not a place because women are out of their places there. It is a house where women are not, according to traditional ideology, at home. And yet women are safe there. They are at home: "even when we dream ourselves alone / and far away we bump against / some small reminder of what we are / left with   live within" ("Signs of the Former Tenant II" *SFT* 64). In our culture, women can be safe only when we are home-free.

"Intervals" challenges the ideology of what the poem calls "love's body / where the prince and the princess live / happily ever after. / Your own childhood" ("Intervals" *SPG* 59). The poem itself is an interval that opens up the possibility of meaning for women by rereading "what we have been given":

> How we've made it seem normal,
> when I open the door at 3 a.m.
> and the cops are there with another one,
> three kids in pyjamas, a few clothes
> in a green garbage bag.
> ("Intervals" *SPG* 65)

Like the name of the place in Kingston (Interval *House*), this poem speaks an absence: "these houses / where language capitulates and love / is something to be beaten / out of another's body / or in" (*SPG* 67). As Interval House itself does, the poem points out the effects of ideology, "the way we've chosen to live" (*AW* 21): "as if there were more than this, our real selves / different from what we make of each other, what we accept" ("Intervals" *SPG* 67).

It is the function of ideology not to recognize the "gap," what is left out, the interval. According to Althusser, ideology ensures "the absolute guarantee that everything really is so, and that on condition that the subjects recognize what they are and behave accordingly, everything will be all right: Amen—'So be it'" (181). Writing at this interval—where what we have been given and what we require "bump against" each other—is a metaphor for Wallace's practice, her feminist critique of ideology, generally.

There is a further paradox. As Wallace acknowledged in an interview with Peter Gzowski, she could not write while working at Interval House:

> PG: Do you recollect in tranquillity?
>
> BW: Yeah (laughs). Because when I was working at the House I didn't write any poems. I certainly couldn't have written a poem about the situation. And in fact one of the reasons why I left eventually was that I wasn't writing at all. And I knew that I had to get back to it.
>
> PG: You really need the distance. ("The Morningside Interviews" *Open Letter* 24)

That split "I" getting back to it, getting the words for it, getting down to it. Where "I" is located and what "it" signifies are the absences in contemporary ideology which, like the "friendship of women," are not "mentioned in hospital policy" ("A Simple Poem for Virginia Woolf" *SFT* 49), in the world that ideology makes possible.

The "I" speaking in *Marrying into the Family, Signs of the Former Tenant, Common Magic,* and *The Stubborn Particulars of Grace* is, as Wallace said in an interview with Janice Williamson conducted in February 1989, "always very clearly a female voice" which uses "female anecdote as a metaphor for human experience" and assumes that "a female view of the world could be a human view of the world" (*AW* 208). Nancy Hartsock makes a similar argument for what she calls a "feminist standpoint" in her essay "Developing the Ground for a Specifically Feminist Historical Materialism" when she writes: "I will focus on women's life activity and on the institutions which structure that activity" (162). By the words "feminist standpoint" Hartsock means "not simply an interested position (interpreted as bias)" but "interested in the sense of being engaged" (159): a feminist standpoint can "allow us to understand patriarchal institutions and ideologies as perverse inversions of more humane social relations" (159).

But it is more than this. The poems interpellate a feminist subject as both speaker and reader. The speaker of the poems speaks at the interval between what is conventionally recognizable and what a feminist critique of meaning makes it possible to see. As readers, we are called upon to take up the position offered to the "you" in the poem; we learn a reading strategy that dismantles the apparent completeness of the ideology we thought we knew. In reading these poems, we recognize what we have never seen before. We become the subjects of feminism. Beginning with the representations of women, motherhood, family, death, women's friendships (all still easily available in white, middle-class Ontario), Wallace's poems open up alternative "ways of seeing."

"Thinking with the Heart," for example, rereads the "patriarchal institution" in the words of a Kingston policeman, cited at the opening of the poem: "*The problem with you women is, you think with your hearts*" (*CM* 59). The poem explores the implications of the clichéd, unrecognized, and ideologically-charged assumption that women do think with their hearts for actual women's lives, for "what we make of each other, what we accept" (*SPG* 67):

> Thought should be linear.
> That's what the policeman means
> when I bring the woman to him,
> what he has to offer for her bruises, the cut
> over her eye: *charge him or we can't help you.*
> …
> Out of her bed then, her house, her life,
> but not her head, no, nor her children,
> out from under her skin.
> Not out of her heart, which goes on
> in its slow, dark way, wanting
> whatever it is hearts want
> when they think like this;
> (*CM* 60)

Wallace's poems both take as their metaphors and narrative material the ordinary words and things in women's lives and interrogate the possibilities (and limitations) of them. They locate, by examining the implications of the ordinary, the material results of ideological assumptions.

The following citation from Ursula Le Guin, an epigraph to *Signs of the Former Tenant* (a title which describes our situation in ideology: we are all living in the "rooms" of former tenants; their signs, our history, shape us) describes the complex relation between the things we have in the world to use (like words, coffee cups, subject positions, buildings) and the way those "things" (like it, a word which recurs in Wallace's lexicon of the everyday) shape us:

> Things you use; things you possess, and are possessed by; things you build with—bricks words. You build houses with them, and towns, and causeways. But the buildings fall, the causeways cannot go all the way. There is an abyss, a gap, a last step to be taken. (*SFT* 5)

These poems make us aware of the ways we are inscribed, articulate the assumptions which underlie our (common) senses of ourselves, and try to "get" (both retrieve and proliferate the meaning of; get and beget) other words for an "it"—an ideology—that shapes us.

In these poems we glimpse what "Intervals" speaks of, equivocally, as the "*open space lying / between two things*" (*SPG* 62). The following lines, from the significantly-entitled poem, "Into the Midst of It," gesture toward the place of the gap, what is not said. Although we are all given words for it, given the maps, "boundary lines, names, that sort of thing,"

> there are places yet
> where names are powerless
> and what you are entering
> is like the silence words get lost in
> after they've been spoken.
> (*CM* 20)

In these poems we read, with the narrators, the signs of the former tenants, the "signs that anyone *can* read" (20; emphasis mine). Wallace gives us signs of change.

2. *Things Touched and Shared*

> and you sit there
> … the two of you
> knowing your lives
> are shaped somehow by things
> you can't touch
> ("Between Words" *SFT* 61)

The first poem in Wallace's first collection, *Marrying into the Family*, begins to touch the things we think we can't touch by acknowledging alternative relationships—alternative "marriages"—women make possible among themselves even within the conventional discourse of marriage. Marriages between women—mothers, daughters, aunts, sisters, grandmothers—are common in this early collection. These women are related (and re-related) in their use of things:

> but what the women own
> they carry with them
> and in their husbands' homes
> perform this marriage
> of things touched and shared
> woman to woman
> back and forth across a county
> They weave beyond blood lines
> the stubborn pattern
> of their own
> particular ceremonies
> (*MF* 48)

Wallace's poems construct an alternative theory of relationship, not based on linearity or correspondence or paternity, but on

metonymy, a weaving beyond blood lines, a "using of the things /
they used" ("Marriages" *MF* 47), but differently.

"Getting Down to It" is a poem which struggles to read for
absences and new relations between things. The narrator of the
poem, looking at photographs of "aunts cousins grandmothers,"
finds that the "photographs remain silent" (*MF* 75). But, the
poem suggests, these photographs of women do not speak to her
because "they did not choose these postures" (*MF* 75), they are not
speaking but rather are spoken. Where they do speak is in "what
they left," which was

> more accidental *things* tossed up
> from the daily clutter
> pieces of china   silverware
> the odd bit of embroidery
> a recipe for plum jam
> *things* they may have planned
> to hand on   perhaps even
> told stories to go with them
> some little incident
> to decorate the *thing*
> and *things* their hands touched
> without ever thinking of stories
> or even of the need for them
> the stories themselves gone now anyway
> each repetition shaping them
> to other people's memories
> so that only the *things* remain
> arbitrary
> ("Getting Down To It," *MF* 75-76; emphasis mine)

"What they left" were signifiers ("things tossed up"), "all" the
narrator now has "to go by." But this is more than enough. The

poem "Things," for example, from *The Stubborn Particulars of Grace*, considers "the way things are" and argues that "it's things that connect us" (96). Like Oscar Wilde, Wallace finds the significance of things in the material practices of ideology. For Wilde, "the mystery of the world is the visible, not the invisible" (qtd. in Cliff); for Wallace "That coffee mug you hold each morning / without even thinking about it / is a mystery" (*SPG* 97).

"The Maiden Aunts," for example, another poem from the first collection, locates the places and things traditionally and currently assigned to unmarried women:

> They are the ones who in Victorian novels
> fade into the pages
> with a discreet hint of lavender
> and though the modern style is robust well-tailored
> though voices are shrill and they hold
> important positions in offices hospitals
> something about them requires still
> a certain delicacy
> shadowy tales of jiltings   grand renunciations
> in the name of religion or family loyalty
> (*MF* 55)

But "something in their faces" seems "incongruous"—the signifier doesn't correspond to the expected signified—"like the photograph / that catches its subject unaware / startles into being / an attitude so unexpected / that the most familiar relative stares for a moment / before she tosses the thing aside turns / impatiently to poems more appropriate / for gilt-edged albums" (*MF* 56). The maiden aunts are "the thing" tossed aside. They are like those "other photographs" in which "unguarded gestures / seem to open to the dark / like renegade flowers" (*MF* 56). In attempting to name, to "startle into being" such an unexpected attitude—women as renegade flowers opening to the dark—the closing image of the poem offers an empowering, radicalizing, and sensuous place for women.

"The Family Saints and the Dining Room Table," a poem from the first collection, *Marrying into the Family*, speaks of what it might be possible for women to want and the difference between those desires and the value assigned to them. The poem begins by retelling the stories "everyone remembers," stories in which women are constructed as beautiful, passive, and dead: "[E]veryone remembers how beautiful they were / the ones who spent most of their adult life / dying of consumption / and how lovely the others looked / laid out with their dead babies beside them" (*MF* 53). An alternative reading becomes possible when the narrator tells, and we are called upon to interpret, the stories no one talks about.

> But no-one talks at all
> about great-grandmother who refused
> to go to hospital for the tumour
> and had two doctors come in
> to remove it while she lay chloroformed
> on her own dining-room table
>
> …
>
> though they remember how her son's wife
> wouldn't have the table in the house
>
> …
>
> so they gave it to the aunt
> who was an old maid
> and she kept it
> which everyone said just proved
> how queer she was for why
> any decent woman would want

a thing like that in the house
they couldn't understand
(*MF* 54)

By reading Wallace's poems, we begin to understand what "they" can't: why that woman would want a thing like that table, a "thing" which signifies another construction of women as powerful, aggressive, alive.

"A Simple Poem for Virginia Woolf" speaks a powerful silence simply by acknowledging the importance of relationships between women. This poem, which "started out as a simple poem / for Virginia Woolf," includes the reader among the *women* addressed in the poem—"you know the kind / we women writers write these days" (*SFT* 48)—and so empowers us to carry out our own interrogations of the possibilities of meaning. By reading these poems, "we" participate in a community of women readers and writers. Although it started out as a "simple poem" which

wasn't going to mention history
or choices or women's lives
the complexities of women's friendships
or the countless gritty details
of an ordinary woman's life
that never appear in poems at all
(*SFT* 50)

What always "intervenes / between the poem" she "meant to write / and this one"—the one we read—are the "ordinary details" of women's lives. But it is in the ordinary details, the things which are so obsessively referred to and spoken of in the poems, that the unsaid, the interval, can be articulated, touched, shared. By "touching" the things that shape us, these poems suggest, other ways of speaking, of being in the world, become possible, thinkable, *thingable*.

3. All You Have to Do[4]

In *Feminism Unmodified*, Catharine MacKinnon speaks of the ways power and knowledge are connected in the seemingly obvious relations between words and things, in ideology. "Having power means," she says, that "when someone says, 'This is how it is,' it is taken as being that way." Moreover, "the world actually arranges itself to affirm what the powerful want to see":

> Powerlessness means that when you say "This is how it is," it is *not* taken as being that way. This makes articulating silence, perceiving the presence of absence, believing those who have been socially stripped of credibility, critically contextualizing what passes for simple fact, necessary to the epistemology of a politics of the powerless. (164)

For Wallace, all we *have* to do things with is what we are given. Yet "it" is what we do with what we have that matters ("[p]ossibility and limitation mean about the same thing" *SPG* 7).

In "To Get To You," a poem cited at some length at the beginning of this paper, the speaker says,

> But what I want you to notice
> are the women...
> We all have the same look somehow
>
> ...
>
> the body carried
> like something the woman's not sure what to do with.
> (*CM* 55-56)

Wallace's poems too want us to notice the women, not just that we "manage it," manage to survive, but "that we make it look so easy": "How many rapes were enough / for those women in Vancouver

/ before they got stencils and spray paint / made a word for their rage?" (*CM* 57). Making words for rage is what Wallace's poems ask us to do too. They give us "clearer landmarks" of that "ancient, immediate war" we call patriarchal ideology (*CM* 56).

If we come to Wallace's poems wanting "to believe it" when "people [tell us] how comfortable it is" (*SPG* 59), we leave them asking just what *it* signifies and for whom *it* is comfortable, knowing that *it* "isn't enough" for women.[5] Unquestionably these poems are written "to get to you"—to disturb and move you. They are attempts at seeing what we don't immediately see, taking what we aren't given, being what we haven't been told how to be. In Diane Arbus' words, "it's what I've never seen before [that is, the ideological assumptions which shape all that we can easily see] that I recognize" in Wallace's poems.

Wallace's poems participate in a politics of the powerless by articulating silences, by reading for absences through uncanny juxtaposition and subtle, self-conscious analysis of the discourses in which they are spoken. Her poems are "a reach / for what we only hope / is there" ("Anniversary" *SPG* 55). They are, like the last section of her last book of poetry, "Nearer to Prayers than Stories," in the particular sense articulated by John Berger, from whom the line is taken and from which Wallace cites in "Why I Don't (Always) Write Short Stories": "Poems are nearer to prayers than to stories, but in poetry there is no one behind the language being prayed to. It is the language itself which has to hear and acknowledge" (*AW* 177).

The woman subject of Wallace's poems writes to make us hear and acknowledge the language within which what we are given is spoken. She speaks at the interval where the ordinary "common" details of "particular" women's lives are significant, where the words are not separated "from the lives they come from," where the "ordinary details intervene / between the poem I want to write / and this one," between the world we are given and what we, as the feminist readers her poems give us a way to be, will accept ("A Simple Poem for Virginia Woolf" *SFT* 50-51).

Notes

1. From "Getting the Words for It" (*SFT* 17). The titles of Wallace's books of poetry are abbreviated as elsewhere in this collection.
2. Wallace speaks of her affinity with and admiration for John Berger's work in "Why I Don't (Always) Write Short Stories" in *Arguments with the World*, pp. 169-179.
3. "Possibility and limitation mean about the same thing," the epigraph to *The Stubborn Particulars of Grace*, is from Flannery O'Connor's *Mystery and Manners: Occasional Prose*. Farrar, Straus & Giroux, 1979, p. 170.
4. *All You Have to Do*, film directed and produced in 1982 by Bronwen Wallace and Chris Whynot in association with Margin Productions Ltd., sponsored by the National Film Board of Canada. Like "The Cancer Poems," in *Signs of the Former Tenant*, the film documents Pat Logan's battle with Hodgkin's Disease.
5. Cf. Eric Savoy, "The Antecedents of It," *Open Letter,* vol 7, no. 9, 1991, pp. 88-99.

Works Cited

Althusser, Louis. "Ideology and Ideological State Apparatuses (Notes towards an Investigation)." *Lenin and Philosophy and Other Essays.* Translated by Ben Brewster, New Left, 1971, pp. 127-86.

Arbus, Doon and Marvin Israel, editors. *Diane Arbus: An Aperture Monograph.* Aperture, 1972.

Barrett, Michèle. "Ideology and the cultural production of gender." *Feminist Criticism and Social Change: Sex, Class and Race in Literature and Culture,* edited by Judith Newton and Deborah Rosenfelt. Methuen, 1985.

Bennett, Susan. *Theatre and Museums.* Palgrave Macmillan, 2012.

Berger, John. *Ways of Seeing*. BBC and Penguin, 1972.

Cliff, Michelle. *The Land of Look Behind*. Firebrand Books, 1985.

Connell, Raewyn. *Gender and Power*. Polity Press, 1987.

---. "Transsexual Women and Feminist Thought: Toward New Understanding and New Politics." *Signs*, vol. 37, no. 4, 2012, pp. 857-881.

Coward, Rosalind. *Female Desire: Women's Sexuality Today*. Paladin Books, 1984.

Davis, Tracy C. *The Economics of the British Stage*, 1800-1913. Cambridge UP, 2000.

Frye, Marilyn. *The Politics of Reality: Essays in Feminist Theory*. The Crossing Press, 1983.

Harding, Sandra, editor. *Feminism and Methodology*. Indiana UP, 1987.

Hartsock, Nancy. "The Feminist Standpoint: Developing the Ground for a Specifically Feminist Historical Materialism." In Harding, pp. 157-180.

Lynes, Jeanette. "Close-ups." Rev. of Bronwen Wallace, *The Stubborn Particulars of Grace*. *Canadian Literature*, vols. 122-123, 1989, pp. 212-215.

MacKinnon, Catharine A. "Feminism, Marxism, Method, and the State: Toward a Feminist Jurisprudence." In Harding, pp. 135-156.

---. *Feminism Unmodified: Discourses on Life and Law*. Harvard UP, 1987.

Mouré, Erin. Public *Facebook* message. Posted 10 January 2020. Used with permission.

Mouré, Erin and Bronwen Wallace. *Two Women Talking: Correspondence 1985-1987*, edited by Susan McMaster. Living Archives of The Feminist Caucus of The League of Canadian Poets, 1993.

Perreault, Jeanne. *Writing Selves: Contemporary Feminist Autography*. U of Minnesota P, 1995.

Rudy, Susan. "Gender's Ontoformativity, or Refusing to be Spat out of Reality: Reclaiming Queer Women's Solidarity Through Experimental Writing." *Feminist Theory*, vol. 22, no. 1, 2021, doi:1177/1464700119881311.

Rudy Dorscht, Susan. "Writing at the Interval." In Rudy Dorscht and Savoy, *Particular Arguments*. Open Letter, vol 7, no. 9, 1991, pp. 100-111.

Rudy Dorscht, Susan and Eric Savoy. "Introduction." In Rudy Dorscht and Savoy, *Particular Arguments*. Open Letter, vol 7, no. 9, 1991, pp. 5-9.

---. *Particular Arguments: a special issue on Bronwen Wallace*. Open Letter, vol 7, no. 9, 1991, pp. 1-134.

"The Morningside Interviews" [Peter Gzowski interviews Bronwen Wallace].
Transcribed and edited by Eric Savoy. In Rudy Dorscht and Savoy,
Particular Arguments. Open Letter, vol 7, no. 9, 1991, pp. 15-25.

Savoy, Eric. "The Antecedents of It: A Poetics of Absence," in Rudy Dorscht and
Savoy, *Particular Arguments. Open Letter*, vol 7, no. 9, 1991, pp. 88-99.

Wallace, Bronwen. *Collected Poems of Bronwen Wallace*, edited by Carolyn Smart,
McGill-Queen's UP, 2020.

Brenda Vellino
"A Network of Relations": Ethical Interdependence in Bronwen Wallace's Conversational Lyric

> *From as early as I can remember it was my grandmother, my aunt, my girl friends, my women friends, female teachers and mentors who spoke the world for me ... When my grandmother demanded to know the last name of any of my friends, when she located that friend within her matrix of who married who etc. ... she was celebrating a network of relationships which constituted her world ... the essence of my narrative style—has come from these women's lives and the stories they told. What I try to do is to recreate their voices, their view of things, their way of telling a story.*
> —Bronwen Wallace, *Two Women Talking* 31-32

At the heart of Bronwen Wallace's poetics is a profound sense of the way our lives take shape in narrative relation to other people's stories and their reciprocal responses to ours. As a result, she developed a poetic voice that was immediate, down-to-earth, and always caught in the act of offering up a good story. Her distinctive poetic gesture is the direct address of the conversational lyric, calling a community of readers into narrative filiation and response-ability. Significantly, she attributes her lyric mode to forms that, for her, constitute female popular knowledge and culture—gossip and storytelling. In essays and interviews, Wallace honours a genealogy of female and familial storytellers that produced in her an aesthetic that uncloses the bounded lyric form—the Romantic and New Critical monologic form—opening it to myriad collaborative voices. She recounts the way her narrative poetics developed around the kitchen sink with her multigenerational womenfolk and around the kitchen table with her working-class menfolk (*AW* 173–6). Two overlapping communities of gender and class, then, inform the matrix of her poetic practice. A third community of filiation is ecological, that of the earth itself. The speaking subject of her poems comes to being in webbed communities—fragile, contingent, and interdependent.

Such a relational conception of the human offers the grounds for an ethical subjectivity—accountable for and responsible to the other's well-being, both human and more-than-human. Wallace's longstanding experience in female and feminist communities such as Kingston's Interval House for women and children seeking refuge from domestic violence, provides a context for her wider ethical engagement.[1] Perhaps because women's social experience has been lived out through the legal, medical, economic, cultural, and domestic construction of their bodies, "the body" and its inscription is central to any feminist theorizing. Wallace is no exception. Her relational subject is an explicitly embodied and embedded subject who seeks accountability to her own particular history as it intersects the embodied histories of those she encounters. From deep attention to the vulnerable body, which humans share with others, grows Wallace's ethical engagement with the body's world.[2]

In the discussion that follows, I draw upon poems from Wallace's *The Stubborn Particulars of Grace* (1987) and *Keep That Candle Burning Bright* (1991) to develop my claim that she makes an important intervention into conceptions of traditional lyric through fashioning an embodied, communal, and popularized lyric. I show how this intersects the larger philosophical project of refashioning the individualist subject of Western public discourses. Through an extended close reading of a suite of poems conveying her experience as a social worker at Kingston's Interval House, I explore the ethical possibilities of a relationally constructed and embodied poetics. Following this, I engage the way she expands upon Flannery O'Connor's maxim that "possibility and limitation mean about the same thing" to offer a poetics and ethics of limitations.

Wallace's relational subject is resonant with reconceptualization called for by selected moral philosophers and ethicists (such as Alasdair MacIntyre, Paul Ricoeur, and Emmanuel Levinas) as well as those conceptualized by ecologists like Stacy Alaimo. In the cultural realm, numerous statements of poetics by feminist, environmentalist, and minority racialized poets reflect the urgent need to rethink the lyric as a form that can carry the weighted questions of social embodiment and historical accountability. An alternative lyric modality simultaneously requires new poetics and revisionist models of human subjectivity informed by, but not subordinated to, postmodernist critique.

Wallace's relational subject compels a formal analogue in her hybrid lyric form, which weaves literary, visual, musical, and documentary media together to break down hierarchical categories of elite and popular culture. By invoking a range of intertexts and forms from celebrated photographs of the contemporary grotesque by Diane Arbus to short stories by American writer Flannery O'Connor; from the music of Joni Mitchell, Ferron, and Emmylou Harris to that of Elvis, Bob Dylan, Van Morrison, the Beatles, and the Talking Heads; from Marxism, grass-roots feminism, anthropology, popular science, and social work to newspaper tabloids, gossip, and women's conversations, Wallace evokes and draws upon the co-implication of cultural representations and popular media with literary and social discourses. Such a porous weave of discourses and modes opens the lyric to self-reflective engagement with its status as a form subject to historical process and, consequently, to new articulations of ethical subjectivity.

In *Keep That Candle Burning Bright*, a suite of poems dedicated to Emmylou Harris, Wallace invokes the popular idiom of country music at the juncture of lyric to further democratize the form, opening up the possibilities of poems as public space. This volume also becomes a site for extending Wallace's long-standing redeployment of the elegy form to articulate a "feminist way of dying" (*AW* 208). Finally, while she is skeptical of the possibilities of lyric transformation, she explicitly offers her conversational poems as "smaller stratagems" (*SPG* 33), rituals of provisional healing and grace, "speaking to the wounded place in all of us" (*AW* 208). Inevitably, such claims necessitate renewed engagement with humanist categories and seeming universals, which she persistently risks. These are questions that are often avoided by many of her academic respondents to date.[3] Rather than dismissing them, I suggest that, in order to negotiate a rapprochement between ethics and postmodernism, we need to revisit the categories and vocabularies of Western political and moral philosophy as these are implicated in literary criticism. It is my contention that, through her conversational poetics, this fierce, gentle, and humble poet from Kingston, Ontario, makes a substantial contribution to our conversations around the subject of ethics and an ethical subject for the late twentieth-century, one that continues to resonate into the 21st century as recent lyric criticism demonstrates.[4]

Towards a Communal Lyric Form

> *A story of yours got this one going,*
> *so I'm sending it back now, changed of course,*
> *just as each person I love*
> *is a relocation, where I take up*
> *a different place in the world.*
> —Bronwen Wallace, "Bones," *The Stubborn Particulars of Grace* 80

In "Appeal," and "Benediction," the framing poems for *The Stubborn Particulars of Grace*, Bronwen Wallace establishes the primacy of the conversational, storytelling mode to her poetics. The particulars of daily life spun out in gossip and anecdote around her grandmother's Sunday table provide the material and aesthetic ground out of which she writes. If there is a protagonist in her poems, it is that of the ordinary storyteller—poet, blood relation, friend, and reader—offering and affirming narrative connection in the twin acts of telling and listening. Wallace's "female narrative form" is constructed by "feats of jump-cutting ... digression, interruption, free association, cross-weaving, speculation, re-examination" (Lee 13). Her conversational lyric is driven by an unruly, non-linear logic of interpolated stories and overlapping plot-lines. As she puts it, "a story of yours got this one going" (*SPG* 80). While this form gives the appearance of spontaneity, like other free verse poems it borrows from the extra-literary mode of everyday conversation to create an artful imitation that serves as a "formal analogue" (Holden 33). Wallace is not alone in exploring the "contemporary conversation poem" (Holden 33); what interests me, however, beyond the fact of such artful spontaneity, which turns on the convention of the speaking voice, are the uses to which Wallace deploys the conversational form.[5]

Jonathan Holden suggests that the conversational poem establishes the "ethos of the speaking voice" by an oxymoronic effect of the ordinary poet in the act of brilliant conversation (33-37). I suggest instead that Wallace's genealogical strategy of "evoking other voices," her reconstruction of poetic voice as "only one voice in a huge community" (*AW* 211), offers a significant intervention into the construction of a solitary speaker and virtuosic monologic voice associated with the traditional lyric. Serving as columnist for the *Kingston Whig-Standard*, Wallace cast her essays, like her poems, in a conversational mode, a matrix for understanding the writer-reader transaction as an exchange of mutually implicated and communally defined knowledges: "Writing this column has also helped me to appreciate how much my readers' response contributes to my work, how much I use what people tell me about a poem or a column in writing the next one ... The conversation expands, grows more complex. It could go on for quite a while" (*AW* 201). In her theory of poetry as a conversational transaction, she joins a chorus of poets and lyric theorists who follow Charles Olson's call to shift poetry away from the "lyrical interference of the individual as ego," set forth in his 1950 manifesto "Projective Verse." Recall the conventions once associated with "pure lyric" in the theory and practice of both the Romantics and the New Critics: brevity and condensation; unity of vision and form constellated around a single speaker, feeling, image, and/or situation; representation of inner life or pure subjectivity; the "cry of the heart" overheard by the invisible reader; intensity of emotion and language; epiphany-like insight into the transcendent and sublime; and the timelessness, and universality of the aesthetic object. Not surprisingly, "pure lyric" has often been offered as the perfect embodiment of the literary, exemplary of high culture. Some theorists, such as those gathered in *Lyric Poetry: Beyond the New Criticism* (1985), have pointed out that such conceptions have positioned poets as aesthetic escape artists. The equation of lyric with transcendence, pitting poetry against politics, risks rendering poetry socially irrelevant, a notion Jewish American poet Adrienne Rich stood against in her essay "Blood, Bread, and Poetry," calling instead for a historically accountable, embodied, and situated lyric practice (178, 183, 187).

Responding to the human rights violations of the twentieth century and the ecological crises of the twenty-first century, poets like Adrienne Rich, Carolyn Forché, Dionne Brand, Carol Ann Duffy, Rita Wong, and Stephen Collis have, with increasing urgency, sought to refashion a poetry of social relevance, a lyric that can carry the weight of the historical, social, ecological, and political.[6] Similarly, selected critics offer theories of these new poetic modes, which they are variously calling radicalized lyric

(Willis et al.), dialogic, multi-vocal lyric (Scanlon), vernacular lyric (Bolden, Willis et al.) and community engaged lyric (Nelson, McGuirk), feminist public lyric (Kinnahan) and ecopoetics (Keller 19-20). Rather than participating in the "death of poetry," these renovations of lyric's possibility are contingent upon its capacity for the dialogic already implicit in its several origins as an embodied form whether you look back to Greek forms or myriad oral traditions informing poetic practices today. For Bronwen Wallace, the revitalization of poetry depends on a renegotiation between poem and world; her conversational lyric enacts a deliberate re-placing of the poem in the public sphere and an invocation of diversely webbed communities within the hybrid forms. In short, Wallace's construction of a conversational lyric mode opens the form to possibilities for deeply ethical intersubjective conversations.

Testimony at the Interval: "We Are That Close"

When I talk of disrupting or changing history, I begin with the assumption that people can change, that we are not totally determined by, bespoken by, the culture in which we live.
—Bronwen Wallace, "One More Woman Talking"

In what is perhaps her most moving, powerful, and compelling poem—"Intervals"—Bronwen Wallace uses poetic testimony to call her readers into ethical awareness of extreme-limit experiences of domestic abuse. The poet/speaker of "Intervals" echoes, but is not identical with, Wallace's own experience as a worker at Interval House in Kingston, Ontario. Across the five numbered sequences of the poem—"Entry," "Free Speech," "ECU: On the Job," "Short Story," and "Departure"—Wallace modulates between subjects of focalization: the poet/speaker as Interval House worker, the women and children who are survivors of domestic violence, variously (dis)engaged witnesses, and the reader-witness. This narrative strategy of multiple focalization, coupled with fluid negotiation between voice registers and first-, second-, and third-person pronouns, effectively constructs a relationally constituted ethical subject.[7] By her direct address to the reader, Wallace takes "us" behind the closed doors of those many might see as "them": Her conversational voice draws us to see our complicity with, and our corresponding need to become witnesses against, configurations of power that are tacitly sanctioned by the silences in social memory. Wallace uses body imagery as an "interval," or a place of negotiation between the body of the woman-survivor, that of the speaker/safehouse worker, and that of the reader-witness. Against the impulse to disembodiment evidenced by the discourse of popular culture and media, Wallace offers embodiment as the grounds for ethical encounters between the self and another.

When considering testimonial advocacy such as Wallace undertakes, I note that speech acts of witnessing are never simple or uncomplicated. In "speaking for" the other, writer witnesses risk redeploying an imbalance of representation and social power in which the trauma survivor is reified as victim and stripped of her agency. As Carolyn Forché observes, "humility brings the poet before an ethical tribunal, a place where the writer must recognize the claims of difference, the otherness of others, and the specificities of their experience. Witness, in this light, is problematic; even if one witnessed atrocity, one cannot necessarily speak about it, let alone for it" (37). In "The Problem of Speaking for Others," Linda Alcoff suggests the following helpful strategies: accountability to one's location as constitutive of our analysis, investments, and speech (7); consideration that one's situation is never fully separate from another's in the delicately webbed histories and discourses in which we are mutually constituted (20-21); attentiveness to configurations of power informing any speech act (22); and sustained reflection on the probable outcomes of our words on the material contexts and beings involved (27). These guidelines provide a model for ethical humility in the always vexed circumstance of advocacy witnessing. Wallace herself mentors such testimonial self-vigilance when she acknowledges the limits of her knowledge and vision as an Interval House worker. In an interview with Peter Gzowski, she discusses her unexamined assumptions before working at the shelter:

> I thought what most people thought, which was that people who got involved in that were sick people [...] that it just happened to, you know, maybe to women on welfare or to people who drank [...] And that it was cut and dried, that anybody who stayed in that situation was an idiot [...] By listening very carefully to the women at the House [I realized] that they weren't totally victims and they weren't totally passive. That they *were* trying to work their way through this situation...
> (*AW* 22)

Building from this recognition, Wallace probes beneath the surface of the woman's bruised head in "ECU: On the Job," to open up the layered complexities of agency and survival that occur in the brain and connect us at the cellular level to a possible future:

> the brain is adding hydro to food
> to first and last month's rent, phone bills
> and cough medicine, trying to make ends meet
> while it keeps the heart
> pumping the blood to her wound,
> food for the new cells,
> pushing her slowly into the future
> . . . .
> ... a future

which includes us all, exactly
as the child growing in the salty fluid of the uterus
includes everything our cells remember
of the long swim in from the sea.

Our future. Though it may be no more
than the last few years of this century
already so full of horrors...
(*SPG* 64-65)

Here Wallace deftly negotiates a kind of provisional universal that implicates this woman's future with our future and the future of the planet. She deploys an evolutionary image, a cellular memory of our pre-human genealogies, to compel recognition of an ecological self accountable to its embeddedness in webbed human and biotic communities. Like other contemporary poets, such as Rita Wong, Wallace's concern with ethical interdependency unfolds into ecological awareness. Her practice of an ecological poetics is most manifest in her body imagery, which persistently reminds us of the material, biological, and chemical elements that we share with human and more-than-human others.[8] This realization is integral to Wallace's refashioning of a relational and interdependent subject. Expanding notions of selfhood open up further possibilities for understanding our mutual interdependency with other humans and the ecosystems we inhabit from which emerges a call to ethical accountability.

While this may risk a humanist position that potentially masks and denies difference and particularity, Wallace takes great care to nuance a working definition of commonality in her concept of the "somewhat collective":

the voice of the narrative poem ... is somewhat collective. I say *somewhat* collective, because I recognize that it is also private, specific to a particular person in a particular place, at a particular time. I say *collective* because I want to convey that it is emphatically not "universal," in the sense of Universal Human Experience ... but we do have a collective experience— collective as in choir or political movement—in which the whole grows from, but does not transcend, its separate parts. (*AW* 177-178)

Throughout "Intervals," Wallace implies that the reader has a powerful ethical function as a co-witness in an intersubjective testimonial transaction. In an interview, Wallace reframes our conventional understanding of confessional poetry as an outpouring of intimately tortured but self-enclosed images in the tradition of Lowell, Plath, and Sexton to consider a form that compels relational engagement:

When we tell people intimate things about ourselves, we are in some way asking for ... support, inclusion ... a healing gesture from the other person ... For me, it's a request placed on the reader to stand in a certain relation to the speaker ... We can tell each other about our lives recognizing that we're going to be inextricably connected as long as we're human beings on this earth. (*AW* 213-214)

Such a textual exchange is an interval of ethical bridging in which the reader is called to respond. It is the reader's task to witness the cognitively dissonant, to carry what has been left unsaid, to confirm that this testimony matters in our public memory.

Most profoundly, Bronwen Wallace's "Intervals" leaves the reader with an uncompromising sense of our co-implication as humans in an ongoing history of gendered violence, along with an urgent need to act for our collective future. In a series of refrains that echo across three of the sequences, she moves us from *hearing* voices on the call-in crisis line ("for all they have time to tell me / before something stops them" *SPG* 63), to *seeing* the survivor's bruise in intimate detail ("Something as small as that. / The time we have left / to see it" *SPG* 65), to *doing* or undertaking urgent action based on our intimate connection:

> We are that close.
>
> Each of us, who are only
> the work of our lungs as they empty
> and fill themselves,
> the back, the arms
> the cells' need, the brain
> where all this happens all the time.
> All of it and only that.
>
> We are that close
> The time we have left
> to do it.
> (*SPG* 68)

The cumulative repetition of the "time we have left" emphasizes both urgency and hope, the balance of a future that hangs on our present ethical choices and investments.

Wallace repeatedly positions the women and children survivors, the advocate witness, and readers as co-witnesses in a mutual present upon which our future depends. Here, as elsewhere, Wallace upholds her deep belief in the capacity for mutually determining personal agency and social change: "I begin, always, with the power of the personal, the private, the unique in each of us, which resists, survives and can change the power that our culture has over us ("One More Woman Talking" 42 *supra*). This vision extends in "Change of Heart" to a man who "beat my friend unconscious":

I'd like to make it
his voice, coming to you
as the one witness you can trust,
but instead, there's only mine.
(*SPG* 74)

Yet she imagines "the night it hit home: / this was it, his one and only life" (*SPG* 74) with the result that he made of the memory of the woman's screams a way of "speaking to the muscles / that control his hands, to the stammer / he thinks of as his changed heart" (*SPG* 75). Such a nuanced exploration of this possibility for responsibility refuses a logic in which a male perpetrator of violence is inevitably outside of the ethical community. Wallace characteristically disrupts one-dimensional responses that limit agency, hope and the conditions for change. In tandem with reconstituting subjectivity as relational, agency itself shifts from self-contained individual acts to those that have consequences and reverberations in the concentric narrative communities in which we find ourselves embedded.

"The Smaller Stratagems. Whatever Works": Towards a Feminist Ecology of Dying

I'm writing to the wounded part of each person, men as well as women ... There's a great line in an Adrienne Rich poem about knowing that her wound came from the same place as her power... It's the denial of our damage, our limitation, our vulnerability, our mortality that's got us where we are.

—Bronwen Wallace, *Arguments with the World* 210

Borrowing Flannery O'Connor's maxim that "possibility and limitation mean about the same thing" (poignant words from a woman who lived with lupus), Wallace offers a poetics of limitation, failures, and losses that seeks to effect healing in individuals and the body politic. Not only does she attend to the wounded and imperfect body throughout her writing life but she also reanimates the elegy tradition to significantly rearticulate alienated Western conceptions of death as a feared final ending or as so transcendent as to be unreal. In Wallace's lexicon this is reconfigured through reflection on a "feminist way of dying" (*AW* 208), an understanding she came to after caring for a friend who died of cancer at age thirty-three. In the last year of her own life, Wallace wrote a suite of poems for country music singer, Emmylou Harris, *Keep That Candle Burning Bright*, that embodies her feminist philosophy of dying. This formulation extends her notion of narrative community, positing an ecological understanding of death as meaningfully carried forward in the lives of the living. Wallace established a practice of starting her poetry readings with a poem by a Canadian writer who had died, such as bp Nichol or Gwendolyn MacEwen, to convey her awareness that community "includes the dead as well as the living" (*AW* 211). She writes of how country music great Gram Parsons blooms "from his dying" in Emmylou's cover rendition of one of his songs "as each of us blooms / from the deaths that nourish us and let us go, the deaths we survive" (*KCBB* 36). Death, perceived by many to be the greatest limitation, is reconceived as a place of possibility:

> One of the things I really notice as I get older is … how important it is to develop a feminist understanding of death and dying in the face of denial and the technological nightmare that the medical profession is built on—denial of the body. There's so much power in the body. If we would learn to attend to the power, we would learn not to fear what our bodies do. It's connected to how we see the body of the earth; by denying that we're part of the body of the earth, we're going to kill it. (*AW* 208)

Here, key elements in Wallace's philosophical and poetic vision are brought together: refashioning a relational self involves a double move of revaluing both the powers and limits of our embodied existence as these are implicated in the ebb and flow of ecological cycles. Wallace also revisits the long tradition of poetic meditations on mortality, along with the conventional elegy form; she suggests the necessity of examining the meaning of death for our lives, while historicizing death in the twentieth-century particulars of ecocide, megadeath, and technological intervention.

Against the grain of a culture of "getting over" death, Wallace evokes a "talking lyric" country lament in *Keep That Candle Burning Bright* to show us the wisdom of "hurtin'" songs, singing the sorrow side of life, and a voice that "sings on, using its breaking to do it" (*KCBB* 18). In the tradition of country blues, Wallace offers her own version of talking lyric, crossing boundaries between high and low culture to offer stories for the road, traded over coffee at truck stops on the highway of life, lyrics to live and die by. Country music itself is already a complex border-crossing form, drawing upon and intermixing musical styles and modes from diversely constituted communities with particular racial, working-class, and regional southern roots: African-American gospel and blues; and U.S. folk forms like Celtic fiddling, Appalachian hillbilly blue-grass, waltz, and ballad. It is a music of grit and survival that connects to my own ancestral lineage, particularly one tough granny, Sarah Bishop, who single-handedly raised eight children on welfare in a two-room house during the Depression era in Alabama. The iconography of country invokes a kind of allegory of the rootlessness and displacement experienced by the subjects of twentieth-century capitalism in North America, along with a call to reground in and seek out new forms of community.[9] From the tropes of country music—truck stops, truckers, cowboys, rodeos, drifters, on-the-road-again songs, hurting songs, drinking songs, break-up songs—Wallace creates poem parables, enigmatic gems that provide wisdom for the life journey.

Wallace's poetry of awkward embodiment—"singing for everything I couldn't be" (*KCBB* 10) facilitates a negotiation between the stubborn particulars of daily life and mystery. It is the invocation of the imperfect body, the out-of-tune voice—those "noisy, untidy selves we've lost, out there somewhere" (*KCBB* 11), the partial gesture of connection that renders her poems so powerful. In their ordinariness, limitations find a place, a voice, to feel at home in and with:

> Why not sing for what we can't do, instead of all this booming and bragging, most of us stuck in the back row anyway, squawking, gimped-up. What if some tuneless wonder's all we've got to say for ourselves? Off-key, our failings held out, at last, to each other. What else have we got to offer, really? What else do we think they're for? (*KCBB* 32)

Here the lyricism of the song is refashioned as off-key "talking country blues" singing for "what we can't do."[10] Humorous and humbled acceptance of failings is the ground note for community formation. This rewrites an ethos of mastery that attends the performance of both the poet, the musician, and often the literary critic.

One section of *The Stubborn Particulars of Grace*, entitled "Nearer to Prayers than Stories," signals another genre-crossing impulse of lyric's ancient roots in communal ritual. Gestures and phenomena that now seem to belong to anachronistic quasi-religious discourses circulate: miracles, grace, blessing, benedictions, saints' relics, and personal talismans. In fact, the poet/speaker seeks to come to terms with the "practical / particulars of grace" at the Sunday dinner table, and the possibility that she could "say for myself, just once, / without embarrassment, *bless*, / thrown out as to some lightness / that I actually believe in" (*SPG* 110-111). For those without particular affiliation to a faith tradition, Wallace's speaker suggests we still need rituals that confer a sense of blessedness on passages of daily life and suggest perhaps accountability to something beyond ourselves. Is it possible that the gifts of lyric might provide some clues: registers of aesthetically composed phrases, images, and language; slowed down modes of attention often meditating on small details; engagement with embodied rhythms and cadence through the sonic properties of poetry? Lyric's historical relation to the mnemonic in its sound devices and the performative speech act points to possibilities for lyric as a form that is potentially non-dualistic in its simultaneous attention to inner life, embodiment, and social memory.

Bronwen Wallace's conversational poetic practice has compelled me to re-examine the contemporary suspicion of categories like the aesthetic, the beautiful, and, even, the transcendent. While we need to remain attentive to the dangers of unmitigated transcendence, which has been so frequently counterposed to the stubborn particulars of daily life and history, perhaps contemporary poets are showing the way for a non-dualistic negotiation between spirit, heart, and social registers. Do we need both/and strategies rather than privileging one at the expense of the other? Rather than the song being elevated above the struggle or the struggle dragging the song through the mud, is there a balance to be found? Like her provisional universal, Wallace asks us to reconsider the possible benefits of a category akin to everyday radiance.

In *Stubborn Particulars*, imagery of the illumined body—bones rendered translucent in an X-ray scan—recalls the preciousness of life sustained in this moment:

> what he sees; how their deaths
> quicken the air around them, stipple their bodies
> with a light like the green signals

> trees send out before leaves appear.
>
> . . . .
>
> but doesn't it come to the same thing
> for all of us? So frail, how could we bear
> this much grace, when it glances
> off the odds and ends we've no idea
> what to do with … (*SPG* 40)

No longer in some elsewhere or "up there," grace glances like light off the odds and ends of daily life, the stubborn particulars through which each of our fragile bodies moves. Mystery—the uncanny, grace-grounded, indwelling in the here and now, incarnate in our biotic and human communities. As Wallace says, foreshadowing her own early death, "What about … the woman who accepts her death and in doing so enriches her life? The whole idea that the body must be transcended—both the human body and the planet's—where has that gotten us?" (Wallace and Mouré 22).

Wallace's relational subjectivity, her lyric community midwifed in the conversational lyric form itself, and her commitment to provisional healing, leaves her vulnerable to critics like Rachel Blau DuPlessis:

> One sees a moving and serious reconsideration of gender in feminist 'humanist' poetries—combined with an attention to wholeness, healing, lyric transcendence, and affirmation that is not a uniformly plausible, though it is always a repetitively narratable, sequence. If one could retain that passionate, feeling ethics without the uniformities of telos… (153)

What critics have failed to notice with respect to much of what gets panned as a nostalgic relapse is that this is not the old humanism. Most accurately, Wallace is a posthumanist humanist. Her emphasis on the dignity of all life forms, including the more-than-human, does not allow for a collapse back into uncritical humanism. Similar to Susan Stanford Friedman (480-481) Wallace reanimates uncritical categories of subjectivity, agency, community, and, most importantly, ethics. Her attentiveness to complex registers of identity, contexts, and construction of knowledge/power indicates implicit incorporation of some of postmodernism's important questions. Feminists and diversely minoritized writers have argued that we cannot do away with notions of subjectivity and agency, standpoint and commitment, but, instead, must renegotiate these, submit them to the lens of self-reflexive critical thinking, and re-circulate them in the context of living practice and ongoing exchange. Wallace's conversational lyric, her relational and embodied subject, and her ethical poetics contribute to a revitalization of poetry, ethics, and community that we cannot live without.

> for a moment in there, maybe two or three milliseconds, your body moves to the beat my thought set up, just as my hand writes by what it hears of you, out there somewhere. You should almost say that, for a millisecond anyway, we both consent to this, with our whole selves, every strand alight and quivering. (*KCBB* 43–4)

Acknowledgments

I wish to offer my profound appreciation to Bronwen Wallace for a poetry of vision, honesty, integrity, beauty, grit, and humour. My heart's gratitude to Robin Buyers for introducing me to Wallace's writing many years ago. Ongoing thanks to several generations of students for thoughtful seminars and essays on Wallace's work. I am especially grateful to SSHRC for research funding, to Naomi Watson Laird for her research assistance, to Barbara Gabriel for her fine editorial eye, and to Andre Vellino for sharpening my mind and softening my spirit.

Notes

1. I wish to distinguish Wallace's ethical vision from an essentialist feminist ethic of care, nurture, and connectedness.
2. This is in direct contradistinction to lyric critic Stephen Burt's recent claim that "lyric poetry disembodies" in that it "aspires to replace the live, mortal, present body.... with 'poetic artifice.'"
3. In a special Bronwen Wallace issue of *Open Letter*, Eric Savoy, Susan Rudy and Barbara Godard each recuperate Wallace for postmodernism and poststructuralism in a manner that does not account for those unruly elements that resist such critical domestication. Interestingly, Wallace herself was wary of approaching writing solely through a postmodern frame (*AW* 206-207). Mary Di Michele, in conversation with Barbara Godard, argues that Wallace was writing "beyond postmodernism" to foster community (di Michele 55).
4. I situate this chapter in direct collegial debate with Burt's engagement with what can only be seen as model of conventional lyric in his extended review of *The Lyric Theory Reader* (2014) which tellingly does not present models of lyric informed by contemporary renovations by many feminist or African American or postcolonial approaches to poetry. Since Burt frequently uses the terms lyric and poetry interchangeably even when he means that the lyric he and other critics have in mind is essentially still that determined by romantic notions of individualist, expressive utterance, I also suggest that Wallace's conversational poetic form is situated within the lyric debates of the late twentieth century.
5. See Donna Bennett on Wallace's recasting of the meditative lyric as the "stream-of-conversation poem" (77).
6. Consider also the increasing popularity of cross-medium performance

forms of dub poetry, rap, and spoken word, which suggests that poetry continues to matter in public culture, even as it keeps on changing to accommodate new audiences.

7. I am indebted to Bina Freiwald's excellent discussion of Wallace's use of narrative voice and pronouns.

8. For further evidence of Wallace's deliberate construction of a biotic or ecological subject, see her poem devoted to Koko the talking gorilla (*SPG* 85), "Rhythm and Genes" (*KCBB* 41), and numerous essays in *Arguments with the World*. While the conjunction of environmental and feminist commitments could lead one to read Wallace as an eco-feminist, she does not invoke the central axiom of conflated violation of woman and the earth so much as she draws upon notions similar to deep ecology's concept of the earth as a life-web and biotic community in which each living being compels biospecies respect (Halifax 25, 34).

9. Interestingly, Wallace side-steps questions of gender stereotypes associated with country music by invoking Emmylou Harris, a female precursor central to the 1970s upsurge in women's country. Further, Wallace seems most interested in country as a form preoccupied with community defined by social class.

10. I am indebted to Dennis Lee's cover notes on *KCBB* for the term "talking country blues."

Works Cited

Alcoff, Linda. "The Problem of Speaking for Others." *Cultural Critique*, vol. 20, Winter 1991-92, pp. 5-33.

Alaimo, Stacy. *Bodily Natures: Science, Environment, and the Material Self.* Indiana UP, 2010.

Bennett, Donna. "Bronwen Wallace and the Meditative Poem." *Queen's Quarterly*, vol 98, no.1, 1991, pp. 58-79.

Bolden, Tony. *Afro-Blue: Improvisations in African American Poetry and Culture.* U of Illinois P, 2004.

Burt, Stephen. "What is this Thing Called Lyric?" *Modern Philology*, vol. 113, no.3, 2016, pp. 422-440.

di Michele, Mary, and Barbara Godard. "'Patterns of Their Own Particular Ceremonies': A Conversation in an Elegiac Mode." *Open Letter*, vol 7, no. 9, 1991, pp. 36-59.

DuPlessis, Rachel Blau. "Otherhow: Poetry and Gender: some Ideas." *The Pink Guitar: Writing as Feminist Practice*. Routledge, 1990, pp. 140–56.

Forché, Carolyn, editor. "Introduction." *Against Forgetting: Twentieth Century Poetry of Witness*. Norton, 1993, pp. 29-47.

Freiwald, Bina. "'This isn't One to Be Told / in the Third Person': Wallace's Life Stories." *Open Letter*. vol 7, no. 9, 1991, pp. 112-133.

Friedman, Susan Stanford. "Post/Poststructuralist Feminist Criticism: The Politics of Recuperation and Negotiation." *New Literary History*, vol. 22, no. 2, 1991, pp. 465-490.

Halifax, Joan. "The Third Body: Buddhism, Shamanism, and Deep Ecology." *Dharma Gaia: A Harvest of Essays in Buddhism and Ecology*. Parallax, 1990, pp. 20-38.

Holden, Jonathan. "The Contemporary Conversation Poem." *Style and Authenticity in Postmodern Poetry*. U of Missouri P, 1986, pp. 33-44.

Keller, Lynn. *Recomposing Ecopoetics: North-American Poetry of the Self-Conscious Anthropocene*. U of Virginia P, 2017.

Kinnahan, Linda. *Lyric Interventions: Feminism, Experimental Poetry, and Contemporary Discourse*. U of Chicago P, 2004.

Lee, Dennis. "A Geography of Stories." *Open Letter,* vol 7, no. 9, 1991, pp. 11-14.

Levinas, Emmanuel. *The Levinas Reader*. Edited by Sean Hand. Basil Blackwell, 1989.

MacIntyre, Alasdair. *After Virtue: A Study in Moral Theory*. Notre Dame UP, 1981.

McGuirk, Kevin. "'All Wi Doin': Tony Harrison, Linton Kwesi Johnson, and the Cultural Work of Lyric in Postwar Britain." *New Definitions of Lyric: Theory, Technology and Culture*. Garland, 1998, pp. 49-76.

Nelson, Cary. *Revolutionary Memory: Recovering the Poetry of the American Left*.

Routledge, 2001.

Olson, Charles. 1950. "Projective Verse." *Poetry Foundation*: https://www.poetryfoundation.org/articles/69406/projective-verse

Rich, Adrienne. "Blood, Bread, and Poetry: The Location of the Poet." *Blood, Bread, and Poetry: Selected Prose*. Norton, 1986. pp. 167-201.

Ricoeur, Paul. *Oneself as Another*. U of Chicago P, 1993.

Rudy Dorscht, Susan. "Writing at the Interval." *Open Letter*, vol 7, no. 9, 1991, pp. 100-111.

--- and Eric Savoy. "Introduction." Special Bronwen Wallace Issue. *Open Letter*, vol 7, no. 9, 1991, pp. 5–9.

Scanlon, Mara. "Ethics and the Lyric: form, dialogue, answerability." *College Literature*, vol. 34, no.1, 2007, pp. 1-22.

Wallace, Bronwen and Erin Mouré. *Two Women Talking: Correspondence 1985–87*. Edited by Susan McMaster. Living Archives of the Feminist Caucus of the League of Canadian Poets, 1993.

Willis, Elizabeth et al., editors. *Radical Vernacular: Lorine Niedecker and the Poetics of Place*. U of Iowa P, 2008.

Patrick Lane
For Bronwen Wallace

Your poems are stories with common bones, cadence the guide
that turns a people into a map of your heart, a history made from
prison stones, everything in the details, letters that asked for grace
and caught it with the lifelines you threw out. We sat out on the
lawn back of the house in Saskatoon, you with your joint and a beer
in the other hand. I used to wonder how you could make sense
stoned. I never could. Two tokes and I'd be under the bed hiding
in a corner like a dustball afraid of a broom. My world was cocaine
and whisky. I could ask how *I* made sense. I don't think I ever did.
You just kept on talking about the women you knew, the ones in
prison, the ones just dead, the ones who were your friends. All that
fragility, the blown glass ornaments that were their lives, you juggling
them in the wind, trying hard not to let them fall. I liked your anger
and your stubbornness, the way you'd tense your jaw as if you had
to worry something in there, some hard candy heart that wouldn't
melt. But all the struggle never gave me you. You kept your tears for
poems. Back in the League days you were always tied up with Mary,
Roo, and Carolyn. There wasn't room for a man. I kept my distance,
watched your feminist moves, and danced what steps I knew in the
suites where men punched each other out or got left in gutters, too
drunk to understand your voice, your quiet rage. It was the common
plight of men who misplaced love, thinking change could be made
with a boyish plea for mercy. You'd seen enough of that, a beer bottle
smashed against a wall, a woman beaten by the man who loved her.
There's only so much anyone can say—or do. This learning to love
is hard and common magic is mostly shared on sidewalks where the
furniture gets piled, in safe houses where a woman finds what love
there is among her kind before going back to the storm. What I loved
most about you was forgiveness and your need to find a common

truth in a common touch. And maybe that's it, a touch and nothing more. I wasn't around when the cancer ate your mouth. I hated my thinking it was ironic a poet could die in the place where words were made. How cheap a borrowed pain in the limits a body is. Rooms within rooms, a lawn and a man and woman talking about Levine and Wayman, Purdy and Acorn, the men you said had given you a place where you could cry the time. Neruda too. And Lowther. It was the fists of men, the women bruised and broken, the indignities that dogged you. But who was it I knew when I knew you? Facts get mixed up in poems and fictions are a poet's safest bet to change a world. You were all stories, beginnings, middles, ends, and the means was in the measure you ladled out. You said, *we carry our lives in our hands*, and we do, an open hand held out to hold another, simple things so fragile even a breath can break them, a word, a poem, the cadence in a woman's voice, like a rocking chair someone's left. It moves by itself a while, then stops.

Editor's Note: This prose poem is part of a series of elegies for Canadian poets from Patrick Lane's collection *Last Water Song* (2007) that appears in *The Collected Poems of Patrick Lane* (2011) edited by Russell Brown and Donna Bennett and is reprinted here with permission of Harbour Publishing. According to the notes to *The Collected Poems* "each contains allusions to the work of the poet being addressed" (535). The line *There's only so much anyone can say* is the opening line of Wallace's poem "Splitting It Up" (*CM* 66) and *we carry our lives in our hands is from* "Learning from the Hands" (*CM* 87).

Lorraine York
"Crazy Detours": The Digressive Activism of Bronwen Wallace

In his moving and intelligent tribute to Bronwen Wallace's life published in the *Globe and Mail*, shortly after her death, Dennis Lee described Wallace's day-to-day life as a kind of digression in action:

> A friend tells of visiting Bronwen in Kingston last spring, before the cancer had shown up. It was a warm Saturday, and they set out on a five-minute stroll to the farmers' market. An hour later they still hadn't gotten there. Every block or so Bronwen would be hailed by a friend or relative, often a generation older, with whom familiar stories had to be savoured, recent news and gossip updated. (Lee 11)

"Merely going from A to B in her hometown," Lee notes, "she was tacking through currents of tribal narrative" (Lee 11). I like Lee's verb "tacking," with its nautical suggestion of a daily sidewinding, seesaw routine in Wallace's lakeside hometown. In this essay, I import this idea of digression, the celebrated back-and-forth tacking movement of Bronwen Wallace's poems, into a context that might initially be thought inhospitable to it: activist poetry, where direct, searing statement would seem to be the *sine qua non* of poetic accomplishment.

In many readings of a poetic career, even one as sadly shortened as this one, linearity and development are sought out and constructed by academics and general readers alike. True, all writers evolve, but the narratives drawn of Wallace's evolution tend to describe a movement from A to B, where A involves a dissection of the domestic quotidian, and B is an explicitly political poetry. Eric Savoy described this path as an evolution from the influence on Wallace of Alice Munro to that of Flannery O'Connor: from what he calls the "Munrovian emphasis on the 'real and prodigal' world" to "the intrusion of the 'real, and dangerous' world of random violence and inarticulate fear" that he sees animating the stories of O'Connor (91). Besides underestimating the "real and dangerous" worlds created by Alice Munro (think of "Royal Beatings" alone, the opening story from *Who Do You Think You Are?*), such a construction implicitly suggests a movement from a soft and fuzzy poetic to a tough-edged extremity. Not surprisingly, Savoy sees the latter world as an explicitly political one; in later collections, he perceives what he calls a "shifting boundary between security and danger" that Wallace moves back and forth across; as she does so, Savoy notes, "her observations are intensely politicized" (96). There is much in what Savoy perceives here— that boundary-crossing in particular (or, rather, boundary-*refusing*, as security and danger come to animate, simultaneously, the spaces that we inhabit, everyday)—but the overall effect is to depoliticize the earlier poetry. In what follows, I propose digression as a major mode in which Wallace writes activist poetry, altering in the process our very ideas about what activist poetry is and does.

But to digress briefly, digression has long been seen as a touchstone of Wallace's writing, and from the way readers describe her poetic "tacking," you can sense their enjoyment of, their delight in her rich indirections; Wallace's method seems to inspire verbal inventiveness in those who simply seek to describe it. "A loopy, lopey canter" (12) Dennis Lee calls Wallace's digression, and Gary Geddes notes that it, like other "old oral techniques" like counterpoint, refuses what he calls "the linear road of yellow bricks … taking instead the necessarily circuitous route to the heart" (391). Donna Bennett devises a striking mathematical metaphor, likening this digressive movement to "the meeting of different oblique vectors" (65) which create in Wallace's poetry not exactly a stream of consciousness but, instead, what she aptly coins "a stream-of-conversation" (71).

When it comes to interpreting those digressions, many possible readings emerge, rather like those oblique vectors Bennett describes. Criticisms from the late 80s predictably saw in digression's deferral of transcendent meaning, a correlative to literary deconstruction's understanding of language and subjectivity; essays by Susan Rudy and Eric Savoy in the special issue of *Open Letter* devoted to Wallace took that tack. But as my own assumption of the nautical metaphor suggests, interpretations of Wallace's poetry have made their own "loopy, lopey canters," and a reaction against that earlier approach is apparent, for instance, in the detailed reading of Wallace's poetry offered by Brenda Vellino. She suggests that attempts to, in her words, "recuperate" Wallace for a postmodern and poststructuralist poetics did "not account for those unruly elements that resist such critical domestication" (114 *supra* n. 3). Vellino explores, instead, the idea that Wallace's lyrics of conversation open up a space for self and other to meet and mingle in a manner that is, at its very heart, ethical. She even calls upon the works of philosopher Alasdair MacIntyre, who sees the construction of a narrative of self as profoundly interactive—I would say, digressive; "human life unfolds as lived narrative with unpredictable turns, formal constraints, and multiple plot options" (Vellino 309).

My own contribution to this discussion grows out of recent moves, by Vellino and by Donna Bennett, to see Wallace's poetry as growing out of and radically revising the lyric. By writing poems that perform the work of conversational exchange, Wallace "offers," in Vellino's words, "a significant intervention into the construction of a solitary speaker, and virtuosic monologic voice associated with the traditional lyric" (99 *supra*). Bennett comes at this challenge to lyric from another direction, seeing in Wallace's poetry a resistance to the meditative lyric in that it refuses to use the material immediacies of our worlds as a portal through which to reach some transcendent generalization about those worlds (63). The very shape and movement of Wallace's *The Stubborn Particulars of Grace* dramatize Bennett's perception: we begin the collection at Sunday dinner at "Grandma's" and that is roughly where we wend our way back to, in the closing poem: "To come back again, / to those Sundays at my grandmother's table / but by a different way" (*SPG* 110). Or, rather, we return to a place that has been subtly displaced by the meditative journey we have been on in the course of this collection of poems, but however changed, our transformation does not lift us out of the immediate. We have been on a powerfully digressive journey and have "come back again … a different way."

Wallace's digressive poetry works similar challenges to and transformations of the activist poem. This poetry has assumed various names, as practitioners and critics have searched for ways to describe a poetry that has pushed the lyric to respond to public and private trauma: political poetry, poetry of witness, testimony, engaged lyric, anti-lyric. But whatever the title, conceptualizations of this poetry have consistently deployed the rhetoric of urgency and extremity. Carolyn Forché, practitioner and theorist of poetry of witness, refers to it as a poetry "that calls us from the other side of a site of extremity" (31). Indeed, much of her discussion of this poetic mode, in her book *Against Forgetting*, has to do with the demands that the extremity of poetic subject matter places upon form and means of expression; she refers to "shattered, exploded, or splintered narrative" (42) as just some of the poetic responses to this urgent material. Shoshana Felman, in her book with Dori Laub, *Testimony: Crises of Witnessing in Literature, Psychoanalysis and History* goes even further in insisting that a desperate subject requires a desperate poetic: "The literature of testimony," she declares, "is not an art of leisure but an art of urgency" (114).

Beyond literature, when we think of ways to describe our own or others' work of activism, often we reach for the same urgent rhetoric; we speak of "making a gesture"; "raising our voices" and generally prioritizing action over speech. As Daniel K. Cortese found in his interview-based study of activists, the category of activists he calls "Emphatics," those who most confidently self-identify as activists, "employ a schema that internally processes *doing* as the core component of the activist role, creating the 'perfect standard' … which other movement participants will measure themselves against" (232, emphasis mine).

We can readily call to mind poems that perform this rhetorical urgency, from Atwood's line in *True Stories*—"Witness is what you must bear" (69)—to the opening menace of Forché's own "The Colonel": "What you have heard is true. I was in his house" (16). Where does this leave Bronwen Wallace's poetry? It certainly does call to us from "the other side of a site of extremity" (Forché 31) and yet more often than not it sidelines the discourse of decisive, extreme action. How can this poetry reconcile vigorous activism with laconic digression?

Let's take, as an example, what I would describe as Wallace's development of a digressive activism regarding domestic violence. In poems like "Thinking with the Heart" from *Common Magic* and "Neighbours" from *The Stubborn Particulars of Grace*, Wallace explores the gap in understanding between what she calls, in the first poem, "linear" thought: the policeman's frustration that the woman who's been beaten won't just, as he puts it, "get the guy out once and for all" (*CM* 60). Wallace's digressive mode, however, meanders deeply into the life of this woman, revealing in its very movement why such linear thinking is ultimately inadequate:

> Out of her bed, then, her house, her life,
> but not her head, no, nor her children,
> out from under her skin.

Not out of her heart, which goes on
in its slow, dark way, wanting
whatever it is hearts want
when they think like this;
a change in his, probably,
(*CM* 60)

This "slow, dark way" of the heart is the way of digression into the particularities of women's lived experience, and tracking it is a profoundly activist gesture. Not content to rest there, however, with the possibility of this distinction between linearity and digression being mapped simplistically and essentially onto sexual difference, Wallace then proceeds, as Jon Kertzer has noted (81), to undo the policeman's grip on his prized linearity:

Everything else he ignores,
like the grip of his own heart's red
persistent warning that he too is fragile.
(*CM* 61)

In conversations and letters, Wallace described the process by which she came to this digressive understanding of domestic violence, and it reveals that linearity, far from being displaced onto an external patriarchal agency, was an attitude that she had to challenge within herself. As she admitted to Peter Gzowski on CBC *Morningside* in 1986, she used to believe that the choices involved were, in her words, "cut and dried: that anybody who stayed in that situation was an idiot" (*AW* 22). When Gzowski asked her what made her change her mind, Wallace's response articulated what I am calling here a digressive activism:

By listening. By listening very carefully to the women at the House, and by realizing that a lot of what I had always interpreted as 'excuses,' in terms of the arguments they would make for going back, or choices they had made about why they stayed—were in fact survival strategies ... And just hearing stories over and over again and seeing people make different choices and seeing them *wanting* to make one choice and being *forced* to make another because something as simple as the mother's allowance cheque didn't come on time. Or one of the kids got sick so they had to go back. Or they didn't get the apartment they had hoped. (*AW* 23)

The cadences of Wallace's response resonate with the digressive movements of her poetry; compare "A Simple Poem for Virginia Woolf":

I wanted the poem to be carefree and easy
like children playing in the snow
I didn't mean to mention
the price of snowsuits or
how even on the most expensive ones
the zippers always snag
just when you're late for work
and trying to get the children
off to school on time (*SFT* 48)

Though such digressions are often presented, in Wallace's poetry, as a sign of weakness ("I didn't mean to..." she writes here, and in other poems, she will introduce a digression in a similarly self-deprecating way: "Or maybe that's not it / at all" (*SPG* 18); "perhaps" (*SPG* 25); "Oh, I know, I know" (*SPG* 53)), the poems slyly show us the sturdy resilience of the digressive. As Jon Kertzer perceptively notes of Wallace, "she combines uncertainty with resolve" (85). Far from suggesting that this uncertainty somehow dilutes the resolve, Kertzer insists that it is a "volatile mixture" (85). The volatility of Wallace's uncertain resolve is exactly what I seek to capture in describing her digressive activism, for it is, I agree, a most powerful compound.

Bronwen Wallace, of course, knew this perfectly well, and she would have needed neither me nor the small army of critics I've amassed in this paper to explain it to her. In recognition of the "Common Magic" conference's determination not to subjugate the voices of writers, activists and local community to that of academia, I will end this essay by considering Wallace's own way of theorizing this digressive method in her work. On several occasions, she appropriated a term from painting in order to capture it: pentimento. A pentimento is, simply, a painterly change of heart. We use the term whenever we find evidence that a painter has altered an object in a painting by painting over it another version of that object. Famous examples of pentimenti are found, for instance, in 17th-century Spanish painter Diego Velásquez's celebrated painting *Las Meninas*. Infrared analysis of the painting reveals minor changes; for instance, the self-portrait of the painter had Velásquez inclining his head to his right rather than to his left. What's significant, however, about pentimento is that it means, literally, a change of mind (it comes from the Italian verb *pentirsi*, to regret or to repent). For that reason, it does not apply to the reuse of canvas to paint entirely different scenes; central to its meaning, therefore, is artistic vacillation. Traces of more than one artistic choice exist, more or less visibly, but simultaneously, on the painted canvas. For Wallace, this was a suggestive analogue for her literature of digression; as she explained to Erin Mouré in one of the letters collected in *Two Women Talking*, about the fairy tale "Cinderella,"

the story itself is no longer 'clear.' This, for me, is part of its power. I think, in painting, it's called pentimento, that process by which several different scenes are painted on top of one another on a single canvas so that sometimes one can see incongruous bits of an earlier view in a later one. (I got this image, I believe, from Lillian Hellman.) (53)

Wallace is here recalling Hellman's second volume of memoirs, entitled *Pentimento*, a follow-up to her first volume, *An Unfinished Woman*. This is exactly how Hellman understood the autobiographical act, as a process of looking back through the contingent layers of a life's choices; as she wrote in her introduction,

Old paint on a canvas, as it ages, sometimes becomes transparent. When that happens it is possible, in some pictures, to see the original lines: a tree will show through a woman's dress, a child makes way for a dog, a large boat is no longer on an open sea. That is called pentimento because the painter "repented," changed his mind. Perhaps it would be as well to say that the old conception, replaced by a later choice, is a way of seeing and then seeing again. That is all I mean about the people in this book. The paint has aged and I wanted to see what was there for me once, what is there for me now. (3)

Clearly, Hellman's autobiographical pentimenti would have been of absorbing interest to Wallace, given her leftist activism and, in particular, Hellman's brave refusal to name names before the House Committee on Un-American Activities in 1952, an act that resulted in her blacklisting by major Hollywood studios for some years thereafter. Wallace had found a foremother, an earlier practitioner of digressive activism.

In her last book of poems, *Keep that Candle Burning Bright*, Wallace returns to a central concern of hers: the strange flash of the spiritual amidst the detritus of everyday life. It's this that she perceives in the religious songs of country singer Emmylou Harris, and the only way she can describe this bizarre layering of the holy and the ramshackle physical is to call upon the painterly technique that has so struck her as an analogue for her method. As she opens the poem, "The Presence of Jesus," "What I want to call *pentimento*, borrowing that word from another world, to show how he shows up here, amid diesel engines, bar stools, clapboard churches, greasy spoons" (33). Such a bizarre juxtaposition strikes her as crazy, like the "crazy detours" that her friends' studies in linguistic anthropology can take her on in the poem "Testimonies" (*SPG* 47) or like the popular narratives that she loved so much culled from the pages of the *National Enquirer*: "Face of God Appears on GE Refrigerator"; "Velvet Painting of Elvis Cries Real Tears at 'Heartbreak Hotel' (But Cheers Up for 'Jailhouse Rock'")". What Wallace learned, and what she continues to teach us, in embracing the pentimenti of lives—our erasures, second thoughts, half-forgotten stories—was to lose a fear of seeming crazy. In the words of her remembered friend Jessie, from "Food,"

> don't be afraid
> to say what isn't finished, what seems
> crazy. Just say what you can;
> we'll look at it together (*SPG* 52)

Works Cited

Atwood, Margaret. *True Stories*. Oxford UP, 1981.

Bennett, Donna. "Bronwen Wallace and the Meditative Poem." *Queen's Quarterly*, vol. 98, no.1, 1991, pp.58-79.

Cortese, Daniel K. "I'm a 'Good' Activist, You're a 'Bad' Activist, and Everything I Do is Activism: Parsing the Different Types of Activist Identities in LGBTQ Organizing." *Interface: A Journal for and About Social Movements*, vol. 7, no. 1, 2015, pp. 215-246.

Felman, Shoshana and Dori Laub. *Testimony: Crises of Witnessing in Literature,*

Psychoanalysis and History. Routledge, 1992.

Forché, Carolyn. *Against Forgetting: Twentieth-Century Poetry of Witness*. Norton, 1993.

---. "The Colonel." *The Country Between Us*. Harper & Row, 1981.

Geddes, Gary. "Bronwen Wallace, 1945-1989." *Canadian Literature*, vol. 124-125, Spring 1990, p. 391.

Gzowski, Peter and Bronwen Wallace. "The Morningside Interviews." *Open Letter*, vol 7, no. 9, 1991, pp. 15-25. Rpt. in *Arguments with the World*, Quarry, pp. 11-24.

Hellman, Lillian. *Pentimento: A Book of Portraits*. Little, Brown, 1973.

Kertzer, Jon. "Bronwen Wallace: 'The Stubborn Arguments of the Particular.'" *Open Letter*, vol 7, no. 9, 1991, pp. 71-87.

Lee, Dennis. "A Geography of Stories." *Open Letter*, vol 7, no. 9, 1991, pp. 11-14.

Savoy, Eric. "The Antecedents of 'It': A Poetics of Absence." *Open Letter*, vol 7, no. 9, 1991, pp. 88-99.

Velásquez, Diego. *Las Meninas*. Museo del Prado, Madrid.

Vellino, Brenda. "'A Network of Relations': Ethical Interdependence in Bronwen Wallace's Talking Lyric." *Postmodernism and the Ethical Subject*, McGill-Queen's UP, 2004, pp. 302-32. Rpt. in revised form in this volume.

Wallace, Bronwen and Erin Mouré. *Two Women Talking: Correspondence 1985-87*. Edited by Susan McMaster. Living Archives of the Feminist Caucus of the League of Canadian Poets, 1993.

Susan Glickman
"Angels, Not Polarities": Poetry and Prose in the Work of Bronwen Wallace

I write both poetry and fiction. So, when I was asked to present a paper at *Common Magic: The Legacy of Bronwen Wallace*, a conference held at Queen's University in March 2008, I thought it would be fun to explore a topic that has a strong personal resonance for me: Why Bronwen Wallace, a poet who repeatedly insisted that she had no interest in writing fiction, ultimately found herself doing so. Why did she have to repeat her lack of interest in fiction so often? Because everyone—including me—recognized her tremendous talent for storytelling: it was the most distinctive characteristic of her poetry. Why did she reject the prospect of fiction? Because she believed that she could do everything she wanted to do with language within the form of what she called "narrative" poems.

Traditionally, what the rest of us (or at least those of us formerly known as Professor Glickman) call "narrative" poetry has been something along the lines of the epic—a long poem recounting the exploits of a hero and how they affect the fate of a nation—or, if shorter, a ballad recounting a natural or supernatural adventure. *Beowulf, The Odyssey, Sir Patrick Spens, Piers Plowman, The Charge of the Light Brigade, Hiawatha, The Last Spike*: that sort of thing. In narrative poetry, the protagonist is seen from the outside because there is a narrator telling us a story which has been handed down as part of communal wisdom, and the sequence is linear, based on cause and effect, leading up to a climax. There's a beginning, and a middle, and an end, unfolding through time.

But in a Bronwen Wallace poem the sequence is far from linear; we circle around a topic, flash back in memory, probe deeper to get at the meaning of experience. As Dennis Lee put it, in the obituary for Bron he published in the *Globe and Mail* on Saturday August 26, 1989:

> It's a loopy, lopey canter through domestic vignettes, childhood memories, snatches of yarning and yack with women friends, plus alternate takes and digressions all hopscotching through lives and generations linked in a rich random tapestry, maybe punctuated by notions picked up from neurology or pre-history, with the whole lit up by passages of luminous musings on the workaday mystery of being human. (Lee 12)

And just as there is no traditional narrative sequence in a Bronwen Wallace poem, there isn't a traditional narrator either: that is to say, there isn't anyone standing outside the story telling it to us in a relatively detached way. Instead we have a persona, seen as a subject, from the inside, speaking in the first person. And even when that persona is telling us a story about something that happened to somebody else, which occurs frequently, she is much less interested in *what* happened than in *why*—and in how the events she is recounting make people, including her, feel.

Poetry written in the first person focusing on the thoughts, feelings, and memories of an individual has always been called "lyric" poetry. Even the Romantics, who wrote meditative odes in a conversational voice, never claimed that what they were writing was narrative just because it dealt with complex ideas in the voice—as Wordsworth put it—of "a man speaking to men" (*Lyrical Ballads* 300). But what Bron was trying to reproduce was the voice of a woman speaking to women and women, more often than men, use stories to explain why they think the way they do and to support their arguments. Women are less likely to speak in generalities and abstractions such as "The child is father to the man / and so it was since time began" (Wordsworth, "My

Heart Leaps Up"); they are more likely to focus on how the boy's childhood habit of picking the chocolate chips out of his cookies and counting them to see what the average number was foretold his later adult career with Statistics Canada. And this model of storytelling is also the model for the typical Bronwen Wallace poem.

In fact, point of view and content are not the only aspects of Bronwen's style that led her to call her poetry "narrative." Whereas feminism, for many of us who grew up in the 60s and 70s, strongly influenced the *content* of our poetry, it had a more radical effect on Bronwen Wallace: it was the source of her poetic *form*. Not only did she address the subject of women's lives, she told it in women's voices—and in the typical style of women's conversations. This was obvious in the poems she published with Mary di Michele, in their joint first book from Oberon Press back in 1980. Both poets burst onto the scene as mature writers; both were committed feminists. And both had their own idiosyncratic voices, very distinct from each other. Mary's half of the book, entitled *Bread and Chocolate*, sounds like this:

> A skinned rabbit sits in a bowl of blood.
> In the foetal position, it dreams its own death.
> I swell quietly by the warmth of the kitchen,
> like the yolk that is the hidden sun of the egg.
> ("The Disgrace" *Bread and Chocolate* 37)

And Bronwen's half, *Marrying into the Family*, sounds like this:

> The man she married
> (against her father's wishes)
> was a good husband but
> a poor farmer
> when times got bad

he put a mortgage on the farm
by forging her signature
in 1927 they lost
everything
("Grandma Wagar's Double Bind" *MF* 61)

Right from the start, Bronwen's poetic voice was a much closer imitation of ordinary speech than Mary's, or any of the rest of us, for that matter. It was less textual, less overtly an aesthetic construct, less image-centered. It used colloquial language organized by ordinary syntax; it didn't rely very much on figures of speech.

Though she was to become much more daring and adept as her career progressed, recognizing that she didn't need to constrain her frame of reference, her language, or even her rhythms, to be faithful to her principles, the intimacy she created in *Marrying into the Family* by imitating the conversational ramblings of one person to another continued to be a defining characteristic of her style. This is true even of her posthumous collection, *Keep That Candle Burning Bright*, published in 1991, where we still hear that familiar voice in poems like "Driving" which begins:

I know someone who insists that Emmylou Harris saved her life the year she left her husband. It was all so crazy, the only thing my friend could stand to listen to was *Pieces of the Sky* and now, whenever I hear it, I see her driving, at night, the tape deck blaring, driving on and on. (*KCBB* 19)

side by side with the more ambitious rhetorical flourishes of something like "Rhythm and Genes" that begins:

We all hear—though we may not be conscious of—the beat that thrums through every human conversation. *Rhythmic synchrony* it's called, our sync sense, which, like the other five, conducts us through the worlds we make of each other, or in this case, sets us dancing in each other's stops and starts, digressions, turns and leaps of thought, hyperbole, lies, warnings, lovers' cries—we move to music, and the scientists who study this sort of thing (sociolinguistic microanalysts they call themselves) can clock the tempo with a metronome, and score it, too, each eighth note, triplet, rest and syncopation measured as a waltz or a square-dance. (*KCBB* 41)

This remained her territory: from "I know" in the first extract to "we all hear" in the second. She insisted on the commonalities, in the things that "we all" share. And this is also another reason she called her poetry "narrative."

In an essay called "Why I Don't Write Short Stories" first published in *Quarry* in 1988 and then modified two years later to become "Why I Don't (Always) Write Short Stories" (*AW* 169-179), Bronwen notes that the lyrical voice, "with its power for taking the reader on an inner journey, is a necessary part of what we are" (*AW* 178), and then she distinguishes it from the "narrative" voice which includes the collective as well as the individual, placing the personal always in a particular place and time. Well, the people in a Bronwen Wallace poem are defined as much by their particular time and place as they are by their characters. The poems of *Marrying into the Family*, as the title emphasizes, show the speaker seeking to understand her place in the world by tracing her genealogy and geography, and Bronwen's later work continued to draw heavily on anecdotes and incidents from the lives of friends and relatives. So when she calls her poems "narrative" she is really saying two things:

1. They are told in a conversational way and rely heavily on stories.
2. They are very specific as to time, place, and community.

Actually, I think that she was saying three things, but perhaps she assumed that the third was self-evident: that is, she mostly wrote poems that were *longer* than the conventional lyrics we were all used to in the late twentieth century, especially the tight little image-driven ones so typical of modernism. And length is, after all, one of the traditional characteristics of narrative poetry. Bron's poems got long because she wanted to tease out all the nuances of a situation. This desire for amplification and multiple perspectives could even lead her, sometimes, to incorporating alternative points of view into poems such as "In My Mother's Favourite Story" from *Signs of the Former Tenant*, which concludes

> I would have her know
> all streets are treacherous and even the best
> loved children forget the rules
> about crossing with the light
> but perhaps she knows this anyway
> it's her story after all and she always
> puts herself in   alone in the house
> her hand on the telephone
> and her eyes on the scattered toys
> so easily abandoned
> on the empty porch (*SFT* 13)

And I believe that it was this urge to accommodate many voices, this understanding that the truth is polyphonic and experiential rather than monophonic and absolute, that ultimately led her to experiment with fiction.

In "Why I Don't (Always) Write Short Stories," Bron confesses that she had to change the title of her essay and reconsider her early remarks because:

> I am, now, writing short stories, but not because I think they
> are the same as, or even the next logical step after, narrative
> poems. I am writing short stories right now because that's what
> I have been given to write. Or rather, that's what I've chosen to
> do with what I've been given. These women just started talking
> in my head; I chose to listen and to see where it would take me
> … I suspect that it has something to do with what Flannery
> O'Connor calls "the mystery of personality." (*AW* 178)

"These women just started talking in my head," she says. Voice
again—or rather, *voices*, plural. And here's the other part of the
key, I believe, to the implicit question of what it was Bronwen
discovered that fiction could do that poetry couldn't: it could
give us *dialogue*. And for my chatty friend Bronwen Wallace, as
for the Russian literary theorist Mikhail Bakhtin, dialogue is not
merely an aesthetic representation of characters interacting and
ideas colliding but an ethical imperative, because truth itself is
multivalent and can only be understood gradually, contextually,
through the free exchange of ideas.

Forgive me for taking a little detour through literary
theory, but quoting Bakhtin when discussing Bronwen Wallace
is irresistible. Bakhtin, like Bronwen, came from a left-wing
political background. Having grown up with Stalin, he became
disenchanted with the binary model of dialectics as a power
struggle between classes or different points of view, because
this view assumed a hierarchy of values and posited an ultimate
truth to be reached at the end of the struggle. He argued that
democracy in literature, as in life, could only arise from what he
called "polyphony" (435): the sound of many different voices
arguing. This is exactly the model of relationship we find around
the table in the title story of Bronwen's only collection of fiction,
People You'd Trust Your Life To, where four women have continued
their monthly dinners for many years. The women actually have

very little in common except what they've shared, but what they share, besides continuity, is joy and affection, and a safe place to talk about things. Their group seems rather arbitrary and, precisely because of that arbitrariness, provides a spectacular definition of the "trust" mentioned in the story's title. After all, it's easy to be supportive of those who are like you, but more difficult when you are Gail the single mother fleeing abuse, and Nina the pampered doctor's wife, and Selena, the blue-haired lesbian artist.

Bakhtin found the possibility for this kind of tolerance best embodied in novels, because the novelist has much less control over her characters than other writers and therefore is less of a dictator. Indeed, if she has too fixed a world view or "message" and manipulates her characters too clearly in order to express it, the novel will not be convincing. He argued that the evolution of the novel was both *representative* of a change in social awareness from a closed authoritarian society to a more open and skeptical one, and also a *model* of such change for other literary genres. He even spoke of the lyric poem becoming "novelized" as it accommodated different voices, self-parody, and layers of reality. To quote directly:

> In many respects the novel has anticipated, and continues to anticipate, the future development of literature as a whole. In the process of becoming the dominant genre, the novel sparks the renovation of all other genres, it infects them with its spirit of process and inconclusiveness. It draws them ineluctably into its orbit precisely because this orbit coincides with the basic direction of the development of literature as a whole. (Bakhtin, *The Dialogic Imagination* 7)

Now, being a poet myself, I disagree with him to some extent—I think that good poems have always had the ability to be paradoxical and hold different ideas in tension. (Think, for example of Donne's *Holy Sonnets* with their tremendous intellectual pressure of faith and doubt in collision with each other, or, just to stick with sonnets, how about Shakespeare's, with their dizzying combination of lust, disgust, and the worship of beauty?) But I do agree that such complexity is something that good poetry and fiction have in common, and that poets who are interested in exploring it further may find themselves drawn to writing fiction as well because of the way it allows them to embody this polyphony, this conflict of ideas and voices, in real three-dimensional characters who interact with, and influence, each other.

Trying to understand the difference between poetry and fiction in her own essay, Bronwen quotes John Berger, who argues that

> Poems, even when narrative, do not resemble stories. All stories are about battles, of one kind or another, which end in victory and defeat. Everything moves toward the end, when the outcome will be known.
>
> Poems, regardless of any outcome, cross the battlefields, tending the wounded, listening to the wild monologues of the triumphant or the fearful. They bring a kind of peace. Not by anaesthesia or easy reassurance, but by recognition and the promise that what has been experienced cannot disappear as if it had never been. Yet the promise is not of a monument. (Who, still on a battlefield, wants monuments?) The promise is that language has acknowledged, has given shelter, to the experience which demanded, which cried out.
>
> Poems are nearer to prayers than to stories, but in poetry there is no one behind the language being prayed to. It is the language itself which has to hear and acknowledge.
>
> (Berger, *And Our Faces, My Heart, Brief as Photos*, 21 qtd. by Wallace, *AW* 177)

Bronwen liked this analysis so much that she used the phrase "Nearer to prayers than stories" as the title for the concluding section of *The Stubborn Particulars of Grace*, which includes

139

wonderful poems like "Koko" and "Things," poems that confront the question of how we embody experience in language. And though she admits to unease with Berger's macho battlefield analogy, she acknowledges the truth that unlike poems, most stories end in victory or defeat—the "agon" or conflict noted by Aristotle, the very first literary critic whose writings have been preserved, and considered by him the chief necessity of plot.

Perhaps this is yet another clue as to what lured her, despite her initial skepticism, into writing fiction: *plot*, the unfolding of action through time, is what stories can present significantly better than poems, even narrative poems, because they have much more space to do so. In fiction as in physics, space and time are one continuum. A poem can, at best, recount the highlights of a story or sum it up, in order to examine those events, themes or images that resonate most for the speaker. But fiction can enact the whole sequence of events, examine cause and effect, explore the minds and actions and speech of all the participants, and this, of course, is its great appeal to anyone as curious about people as Bronwen Wallace was. The felt reality of lives lived through time affecting each other, of different people with different histories, agendas, feelings, and needs accommodating each other, is something that fiction can achieve more easily than poetry.

So, although she insists that she did not turn to writing stories because they were the next logical step after her narrative poems, I believe that she did. She heard too many voices to fit them all into a single poem or even a long poetic sequence; she needed space and time to develop their implications and explore them fully without the sense of formal constraint that is the challenge and glory of poetry and the lack of which makes fiction more capacious and flexible but often less satisfying to write. And now I should admit that I'm speaking from personal experience. But what I've learned from writing both poetry and fiction is that they are *not* opposites; each genre has the same ingredients. Sound and sense and rhythm.

Place and time and people. Ideas and images. The difference is really just one of proportion.

Hence the title of this essay, "Angels, not Polarities," taken from another of Bronwen's epigraphs, epigraphs which were signposts to her own thinking, as well as a way of bringing even more voices into the conversation. This particular epigraph introduced her only book of short stories, *People You'd Trust Your Life To*, and therefore should be a reliable guide to how she wanted us to understand her project in writing them. It comes from a poem by Adrienne Rich called "Integrity" and reads as follows: "Anger and tenderness: my selves. / And now I can believe they breathe in me / as angels, not polarities" (Rich 8-9).

There's an oblique link to the epigraph in the book itself at the end of a story called "An Easy Life," which goes back and forth between two characters: a guidance counselor, and a girl who is trying to decide whether to break up with her boyfriend and go to college instead of getting pregnant while still a teenager like both her alcoholic mother and her alcoholic grandmother did before her. The older woman is reflecting on her own life while cleaning house and listening to music when suddenly she recalls the feeling of the younger girl's fingers on her face, applying makeup a little too roughly. "Anger and tenderness. From nowhere, Marion feels the tears start. On the Walkman Patsy Cline is singing those songs that someone sings when they've been ditched, trying to cram a lifetime of pain into every note" (*PYT* 118).

Anger and tenderness are "angels, not polarities" because the same fingers convey the double message at the same time. Because we are all full of contradictions, and any literature faithful to our complex human experience, whether it is poetry *or* fiction, must be able to encompass all our contradictory feelings, and all the many voices that articulate our world.

I started out with different theories, more akin to those John Berger suggests in the piece Bron herself quotes: that poems are timeless and fiction time-bound, that poems are about language and fiction about plot, or as she put it herself in a brief suggestive comment in an interview with Janice Williamson, that poems are not about what *happens* but about what is *discovered* (*AW* 210). But a simple question from a student at Queen's last month when I was doing my own reading here challenged my thinking. The student asked me what the difference was for me between writing prose and writing poetry and I found myself replying, quite unexpectedly, that it was dialogue, because both prose and poetry are otherwise primarily textual. When I returned to Bronwen Wallace's work after that insight I saw how hard she had tried *not* to appear textual, to always give the illusion of a speaking voice. And suddenly I began hearing her voice very clearly in my head, as I had not done for some time, and whether it was an auditory hallucination or a ghostly visitation I don't know, but I welcomed it. And then after rereading her stories, and writing the first draft of this paper, I went back to *Arguments with the World* and found her saying this, the February before she died: "I feel very strongly that my voice is only one voice in a huge community. It's very important to remember that this community includes the dead as well as the living" (*AW* 211). I am glad that our conversation with Bronwen Wallace continues.

Works Cited

Bakhtin, Mikhail. *The Dialogic Imagination: Four Essays*. Edited by Michael Holquist. U of Texas P, 1981.

di Michele, Mary. *Bread and Chocolate*. Oberon, 1980.

Lee, Dennis. "A Geography of Stories." *Open Letter*, vol 7, no. 9, 1991, pp. 11-14.

Rich, Adrienne. "Integrity." *A Wild Patience Has Taken Me This Far*. W.W. Norton, 1981.

Wordsworth, William. *Lyrical Ballads*. 1802. Routledge Classics, 2005.

---. "My Heart Leaps Up." *The Golden Treasury* edited by Francis T. Palgrave. 1875. Bartleby.com https://www.bartleby.com/106/286.html

Phil Hall
Twenty Lost Years

Two brothers start school—the teacher asks their names—*Lester B Pearson-Smith*—*John Diefenbaker-Smith*

Really—well—that couldn't be their names—but they insist—so the teacher calls the mother

That's right—says the mother—*when I had the boys*—*I wasn't married*—*& I couldn't think of a better pair of names for a couple of bastards*

*

Voice is a solid—a volatile solid

Our speech—like stone & clay—is a *time-biased* medium—Harold Innis says

It endures over time—& is traditionally associated with what is customary—sacred—moral

Speech is a time-biased solid because it requires & nurtures the stability of a community by actual human interchange

Face-to-face know-how—passed down orally—from one person you'd trust with your life—to another you wouldn't trust as far as

There is no dialogue between sentences—Bakhtin interjects

Utterance not sentence

*

*For Innis—the organization of empires seems to follow two major models—
the first model is militaristic & concerned with the conquest of space—the
second model is religious & concerned with the conquest of time*
(DAVID GODFREY)

*

Innis argues that while the oral tradition is time-biased—flexible
—yet a solid

The written tradition—from papyrus to pop-up—is rigid &
impersonal—*space-biased*

He warns us about an advertising-driven media obsessed by
present-mindedness—*& the continuous—systematic—ruthless
destruction of elements of permanence essential to cultural activity*

*

Marshall McLuhan refers to Innis's *mosaic* writing style

The interaction of substances in a mutual irritation

*In writing—the tendency is to isolate an aspect of some matter
& to direct steady attention upon that aspect*

In dialogue—in contrast—there tends to be an *interplay of
multiple aspects*

*

Tongue on paper—voice—not invoice

Bronwen Wallace knew instinctively what Innis & McLuhan explain

She understood the good balance to be struck between talking & writing—(the letter)

Between speech & text—(the lyric)—between oral history & the document—(Livesay's *Documentaries*)

Sigmund Freud died of cancer of the mouth—as did Ivan Illich —& Bron

Psychoanalysis—Liberation Theology—*our kinda talk*

The tongue is a stele—lash & groove

*

Bron Wallace came knocking—up our back stairs—the night my son was born

Raspberry leaf tea—for the contractions—she said to my wife—Cathy

Look at this poem—she said to me—a typewritten page

It was the one we all know now—the one she ends by dipping her cigarette in her coffee & starting to write

*

Gary Snyder says—it doesn't matter where you draw the line— your line—the important thing is that you draw one—that you won't cross—like in Westerns

He says—when you do that—your little mark in the sand instantly
links up with all of the other lines that are being drawn—they
amount to one line

A unified front against bad food—bad government—bad water—
bad writing—(the cheating arts)

But I didn't learn this from Snyder—I learned this from Bron—
she scraped (& wrote) many lines that she stood behind—many at
once

*

When I met her—I was still scrambling to maintain physical &
mental autonomy—balance enough to call myself a poet

Bron was doing shifts at a collective political bookstore—&
at a parent-run day care that she had helped found—she was
enthusiastic about Lamaze birthing methods—having recently
laboured a child that way—Jeremy

She was arguing regional politics along with national integrity
over beer

Her partner—Ron Baxter—worked for the Post Office—nights—
he had organized a discussion group—they met on break—their
texts were the journals they sorted & borrowed—read—discussed
—& then sorted back into the system

We lived in the same house for a while—in Windsor—upstairs
& downstairs apartments—we were in the same graduate poetry

workshop run by Eugene McNamara at the University of Windsor

*

Maybe I was her first poetry editor—because that year
(1977) I edited the student literary journal—*Generation*—an
embarrassment—except for Bron's poems

She had been drawing so many lines for so long that when she
came to *writing* some they came out full-blown—ripe—sure

She doesn't seem to have known she was a writer until she *was* a
writer—a good one—with almost no embarrassing juvenilia to
stumble through

*

I have built a way forward with poems using doubt

But I have Bron's absolute confidence in all of us with me each
day as I tinker

She believed in a unified front against despair—because she did—
I do—mostly

Sometimes—even now—20 years later—when I've finished a
poem—or think I have—I think—*Bron would like this*

Or—*I'd have a fun old time arguing with Bron about this one*

*

She was no saint—she could be blunt or crude or goofy—hers was an awkward beauty—absent of diversion

Unbudgeable communal faith together with usual-headedness—
she had all that—as her poems do

I write poems so that if she were to knock again—I'll have some

*

The 1957 election was the Canadian people's last gasp of nationalism

George Grant—in *Lament for a Nation*—tells how Diefenbaker &
his Conservative government—between 1957 & 1963—made the
last charge in defence of Canada as an autonomous nation

But by then—Grant says—it was a done deal—*for twenty years before
its defeat in 1957—the Liberal party had been pursuing policies that led
inexorably to the disappearance of Canada*

I would frame Canadian nationalism's decreasingly hopeful
heyday between Diefenbaker's first huge majority election win
that year & a final symbolic knell in 1994 at the signing of the
NAFTA agreement

Mulroney & Reagan singing together at the White House

(The windfall of Canadian literature in the '60s & '70s—was a
crop from an already toppled tree)

*

Bron was born in 1945—she was 12 in 1957 when Diefenbaker
came to power—she was 23 in 1968—she began publishing in the

'70s—she died in 1989

She coincides with Canadian literary nationalism—was a believer
—the last fresh carrier of our optimism—an activist

But not an idealist—she was too *time-biased* for that

*

Everyone at once who was standing on poems then heard
Wallace's voice—we were invigorated by its widening patterns

She carried her regionalism so effortlessly—made it sound
encompassing—place & voice—wherewithal & come-to-roost

Just maybe hers was a voice that could represent us—especially
women—carry forward the tattered standard

Unite us in its humanism—like Purdy's but a woman's—like
Livesay's but funkier

*

Then the voice rotted out from under us & was gone

No one since has tried to speak as familiarly to us—in poems

No one will—no one wants to anymore—it's every poem for itself

The New Internationalism has no time to sit down & yack

*

When a Wallace poem says *I*—it means *me Bronwen*

That's not cool anymore—but that's what she was leading with—herself—herself *among*

Of course her *I* also means *this woman you know who is like yourself*

Her *I* is both herself & a character much like herself—like you & me—men too

A mask—but not a stage mask—not designed or styled—more of a no-make-up-on-yet composite

A hopeful & complex human sort we would all like to see a bit of ourselves in

The woman who is the poem is a mixture of intrigued & baffled—alone & surging with company—an anecdote-hound

Get in here for god's sake & tell me all about it right now

*

We know Bron when we hear her—but we also know now that the first person pronoun is a floater—it hovers—nowhere—it is not the poet

No—it is not the poet—soon after Al Purdy dies he stops sounding like *the voice of the land*

He isn't around to sustain his poems with the legend of his personality

(A trademark swagger of indifference—that bluff & huff—drops away—we fall from shrug to *gravitas*—& the poems—almost embarrassingly—open their profundity)

No—it is not the poet—Wallace's poems too have begun to ring hollow

If she came to class & read to students her poem *Gifts*—the one where her son is crying upstairs during her birthday party because he has bought her a t-shirt that is not *her* & too small

Sure they'd get its complexity of emotions—they would hear how it is about

But there's been a shift—& this is not only pronouns—this is the dilution of political *savvy*—a redefining of *citizens* as *consumers*

Where students used to be eager to discuss their own kids or memories—the whole nature of gifts

They now get into a discussion about—*why doesn't she just return the stupid shirt*

Which will lead to marketing & easy online return policies—(I'm not kidding)

*

The comfort of a friend in a poem—is an illusion

No solution or agreeable shrug—no roundedness or summing up

The Cold of Poetry—as Lyn Hejinian puts it

Yes—closure can be an immense larynx-trap—a reactionary *cul de sac*—as Bron knew too

But we miss our friend—even as we float our pronouns—even as we seek non-closure

The inclusive comfort of what's shared (besides language) has been foregone

We miss a voice like Wallace's—she was good at intense associations followed by you-&-me-both-pal smiles

*

We all know that if Bron had lived she would have become a novelist

For her—as with so many of our best poets—the poem fast became too constraining

Her last poems seem to have endings imposed on them—they want to keep going—talking all night

Therefore—the prose poems—the columns—the short stories

Who inherits her voice—who keeps its perspicuity going

I read to find the traces of her—& each time I hear her tone in poems she didn't write—I like to think we aren't completely hopeless

That our story-pulse may be volatile yet

*

In 1951—Margaret Avison wrote a public school textbook—a
history of Ontario

(Avison born 1918—Edith Fowke 1913—Dorothy Livesay 1909—
Helen Creighton 1899)

In 1951—letters were a sort of money—they were saved—re-read
—inherited

Diaries mushroomed with ink splotches—Bron was six—her
grandmothers were busy—gathering & listening—curious &
inclusive

*

We learned to read from *Readers* that were Grey Owl-ish—British
in tone but including Canadian themes

We were given covers for our *Readers*—paper placemats we folded
as instructed—the front & back panels of a book slid into sleeves

Here's one of those jackets—blotter-paperish—blue—a map
of Northern Canada—the Yukon & the Northwest Territories—
regional crests

Plus a third crest—a *Coca-Cola* symbol—*Northern Canada—Our
Rich Frontier—you may be one of the pioneers of the new North*—a bottle
of Coke

A *Roads to Resources* program—the DEW Line—a cover—for a
book—sure—but its enthusiasm about the North is a cover for
economic take-over too

A promotional gift—propaganda for a done deal—the line blank
where a student might write her name—as if joining some corps

*

For Bron—it's not just—*once upon a time*

She can't tell the story without telling how it is being told

I hear my friend Rhonda reading her daughter Alice to sleep

Once upon a time there was a fish who granted a man three wishes

As I am trying to remember what the wishes are—I hear the train go by

And think of John Fogerty—Big Train From Memphis—he means Elvis

*Once Alice is asleep—her mom & I will talk about our troubles—again—
late into the night*

*The night—which is a whole other story altogether—or the same one but
looser*

The jumble we just can't throw out

*

Why not—well—if it weren't for this narrative jumble—told &
retold—despair would flare through—unmuffled

Almost everyone in Bron's poems has cancer—something hunts
us down & wins even as we defy the odds

Cancer is a train you may not be on today—but you will probably get on board—eventually

So put on Emmylou Harris—or Elvis again—get on that big train—*& ride*

Even the way folks talk about their cancers—is *kinda* optimistic—in a resigned way

Like—*I have to go to Montreal for the weekend—can you feed my fish* while I'm away—like that—& we will—we did—we are

Though the magic is dead inside the wishes—& the tracks empty

*

As you can see—one of Bron's talents was for weaving disparate types into community—*the interaction of substances in a mutual irritation*

Twenty years later—we who knew her—we who only know her by loving her poems—are in this far-flung ditch together—a vinyl (blue flickering) groove

Though the possessive plural—*our*—is increasingly debatable—even from ethnic or class perspectives

Where can people learn independent views—when newspapers & *television throw at them only processed opinions* (GRANT)

Bombarded by business-as-heroism—we crouch—our ears blown —or numb

A laugh track has been synchronized to our *lack of transparency*

Mumbling—*once upon a time*—we deny having heard the call to
full surrender

*

I'm not nearly as optimistic as Bron was—those are *NAFTA geese*
I hear

We've changed since she died—our poems have changed

(And yes—change is health—not writing the same poem means
we out-make palaver)

(And yes—process—going-making—is more essential than
product—the little square ones)

When I try to explore how Wallace's voice has evolved—I mean
I wish it could have

Cheap survivor guilt—I know—for getting on with all this slower
dying without her—poems otherwise—muddling through

*

*So the teacher calls up the mother—& the mother says—I couldn't think of
a better pair of names for a couple of bastards*

I always hear that joke told in Bron's voice now—& it makes me
grin

Aritha van Herk
Ghost Narratives: A Haunting

People You'd Trust Your Life To:[1]

People you'd trust your life to:

people you'd trust your life (story) to:

people you'd trust your story to:

people you'd story your life to:

people you'd trust your people to:

people / life / story:

trust:

the stubborn particulars of trust:

and story:

There is a ghost in Wallace's stories: moving the words around when she isn't writing: when the story isn't telling: when the reader isn't reading. And even when you (the reader) are watching, watching hard: concentrating: the ghost wafts past a line: a paragraph: and vanishes into the framing margin. There is a faint whiff of citronella: the *petit mal* hesitation of almost imprintment: a shadow. Something: a shape: a gesture: something there on the peripheral version of the story.

Wallace's fictional ghost is not a presence discussed at length in narrative theory: by narrative theorists. It is too ephemeral to elementize or define: its haunting too elusive to be made part of the peregrinations of Russian formalist theories; or Bakhtinian (dialogical) theories: or New Critical theories: or neo-Aristotelian theories: or psychoanalytic theories: or hermeneutic and phenom-enological theories: or structuralist, semiotic, and tropological the-ories: or reader response theories: or poststructuralist and decon-structionist theories: of narrative that is.[2]

Wallace's is no literal ghost: no left-over remnant of some character in a rear-ended story: no fictional ghost harassing a fictional character. *People You'd Trust Your Life To* evokes the ghost of story haunting the very story that it attends: fiction's inversely ethereal presence: like a shadow's person.

Narrative suffers the affliction of having to bear too many materialist determinations: "in fictions we order or reorder the givens of experience. We give experience a form and a meaning, a linear order with a shapely beginning, middle, end and central theme."[3] And, what, asks Wallace: in her stories: are the "givens" of experience? Are there any? Are they doing what we pretend they're doing: in either life or fiction? And are those givens somehow responsible: for the ghosts of stories haunting stories?

Whose master narrative has determined that narrative should be boiled down to plot and character: setting and theme: structure and temporality? How is it possible to plumb the "deep structure" of story without consulting its ghosts? And how to consult its ghosts if they are unacknowledged, if a narrative presumably needs only: protagonist, antagonist, witness.[4] Nothing shadowy moving in the wings of the page. Let alone any notion that the story might have a presence beyond itself; elided: extradialectical. The *story* you'd trust your life to is ambivalent: doubly-uncoded: full of loopholes.

But Wallace's fiction refuses to position itself as icon. It refuses the grammar of formatting. It is wilfully corrupt: inconsiderate. It haunts itself. Here is Wallace's narrative problem: *where is the story people can trust their lives to*? Her serious and fictioned question gestures towards the deepest preoccupation of all narrative but usually attended secretly: as lacuna: as absence. Except here, in *People You'd Trust Your Life To*, where Wallace offers a tentative extension: the hand of a ghost held out to fiction.

Wallace haunts her stories. Her stories haunt her stories, each other. They haunt their haunting of themselves. The economies of fiction on the lam: narrative on the loose. Mobilized: refusing to succumb, refusing to exclude, arguing its own discrepancies. Theories of narratology be damned: every narrative contaminates the presumed master narrative: in *People You'd Trust Your Life To* there is at least space accorded to story's permeation of itself.

Story Ungoverned

Wallace reading between the lines: space and italics: making them speak: tender towards the story. Her poet's gesture of ghost lines: the narrative beneath: acting as its own double: questioning its presumed answers: refusing to be managed. The slipstream story. Lydia, in "Chicken 'n' Ribs" enacting a mirror narrative: language that she cannot quite control or restrain: language that is not language but "*whatever*" (15): insinuating its strangeness into the dominant narrative: surface normality: the ostensibly seamless order of events. Which is only that of a woman eating a meal: with her three children: in a Swiss Chalet. How pedestrian can a plot pretend to be?

The story's ghost is an insistent undertone that makes itself heard past the background noise in the restaurant: "*And it serves you right, too, fuck-head*" (24). Its dazzling irreverence: "*Christ, there should be laws against this kind of bullshit*" (22): uncontainable inappropriateness: is the ghost of Lydia's story speaking for itself: sliding into the text and announcing itself the way that Lydia would like to: in her imaginary speeches:

Suddenly, she wants to stand up in front of everyone, tap her coffee cup with her spoon, make an announcement.

"*I'm Lydia Robertson. These are my two eldest children, Richard, who plans to become a mechanical engineer, and Karen, my only daughter, who will study marine biology. Save the whales, maybe, or the whole ocean. I have raised these two, along with their younger brother, Tony, on my own for the past fifteen years, while at the same time finishing my high-school education and becoming a nurse. I am now a supervisor of nursing in the OB unit at the General. I want you to know that I have accomplished all this, alone, with minimal help from my family and without any assistance, other than the obvious and easily performed biological one, from my husband, Ken, a no-good bastard who, who…"* (31)

Her story's spectre goes so far as to almost-intrude on the story: speak past the silencing master narrative of expected behaviour played out in a family restaurant. And the ghost of Lydia's story: with its sub-text of Ken's story: his note as inside story: ("Inside the lunchbox was a plastic bag full of marijuana and ten 100 dollar bills."):

Dear Liddie,

   Look, I'm sorry, but I can't take anymore of this. I've got to get out while I can. I hope what's inside will get you through the worst of it. You can tell the kids whatever you want. I won't be back. Don't try to find me. Please.

   love, Ken (21):

haunts Lydia. She tells the kids: "Daddy isn't coming back" (23): but at the same time, she *cannot* tell the kids: "whatever she wants": they keep telling her (now that they are almost grown): how weird she is: to control herself.

Lydia is excluded from her own story: trapped by her never having spoken her secret self: by her "one and only life, whizzing by her as if, after Ken left, it had no time for her" (29). Lydia's "spiritual experience": her desire to speak past the overt story: is prompted by her story's ghost: her life's haunting. When she says Ken's name aloud (32): and begins to articulate her effaced story: she is freed from the rigidity of her prescribed family narrative:

she is then free to buy every flower in the shop and step into the "other" wedding story that she witnesses in the restaurant: that she is so interested in as a shadow story of her own. Lydia: "laughing and laughing as she enters the small pause where everyone seems to be waiting for her" (33): is a ghost made flesh: her own story come to life: escaping the plot she has always been limited by and walking through an open door: into a story she can trust her life to.

Story Censored

But more than unrestrained story, Wallace grapples with forbidden narrative; not only restrained or unrecognized but deliberately suppressed narrative: censored: never legitimized: and yet it too a ghostly presence on the verge of making itself visible. This story that haunts the patriarchal master narrative: clots together power, abuse, and sexuality: terrible spirits rebelling more and more against the set and established pattern of narrative.

There are no givens in the chaotic grammar of sex: the very refusal of the male master narrative to give sexual stories substance if their originators are women: these stories approach themselves through an insubstantial moment. Like Mr. Simpson in "Fashion Accents" whose "voice was smooth and patient, like chocolate syrup and him just pouring it on until he'd coated everything" (50): the narrative of sexuality is haunted by its own censorship, the thick sweet chocolate syrup of patriarchal obfuscation. In "Fashion Accents" Wallace incorporates the very problematization of the presence of sexuality by effacing it: wrapping it in nail polish and lipstick: Stella's scarves and heels and indefinable style: again present of absence, an unstated narrative:

> Stella's nose was too large, her eyes too close together, her mouth was crooked. But she was beautiful, Stella. Even then

> I knew that her beauty had to do with what was called style. I also knew that I needed some badly since I was not going to be beautiful in the normal, easy way that some of my girlfriends seemed to manage.... I was awkward and skinny; my hair was too straight to be left casually alone. I needed style. At the time I thought it was something simple, something you could learn by watching. (37)

Physical style: like narrative style: intangible: a ghost presence between the lines of actual appearance and illusion. Style enacts Hutcheon's incredulity toward metanarrative:[5] is, in effect, the element that must negotiate the fixations of narratology.

Stella contaminates Brenda's "givens": those that have been imposed on her by her upbringing: her parents: her limited experience. At exactly the narrative moment that Brenda is poised on the brink between eagerness and fear at her developing sexuality, Stella introduces the possibility of multiple and different narratives:

> I was beginning to see that there were a lot of ways of doing things, of living, that I'd never really thought about. My parents made it seem like there was only one way and up until now I had accepted that, at the same time as it made me feel rather, well, *discouraged*. So when I say that Stella suddenly made my life seem possible, what I really mean, I guess, is *possibilities*, ways of getting on that I thought I could manage. (44)

Narrative magic: the story doesn't have to follow the same pattern all the time, there are differences ghosting themselves as possibilities.

Indeed, the very story of the story of the story is ghosted in "Fashion Accents" by Stella's husband, who acts as pimp for the model narratives of movies: the movies that Stella and Brenda go to together: where they are free to react to those implanted / imposed narratives by holding each other and crying for fictional tragedy:

> They seemed so vulnerable, those women on the screen, and so grown-up at the same time, running towards or away from some huge, terrible event. I supposed it was really myself I was crying for then, wanting my own life to be as huge and as terrible as theirs. (48)

Brenda wants her own life-*story* to be as huge and as terrible as the life-stories of the women on the screen. She does not want the articulated but diminished life of her mother: who insists that childbirth is the most quickly forgotten pain in the world but who is unable to reconcile her officially tempered version with her "real" memory of the horror of her giving birth to Brenda. And when Brenda's mother does succumb to the story her memory insists on relating, it is a story that Brenda can only overhear as a ghost: an unknown presence (just back from the high-pitched tension of discovering her own sexual narrative): caught on the landing between floors (or pages).

In laconic circularity, Brenda's overhearing of this terrible story, so unlike the model narratives imposed on childbirth and sexuality, evokes the ghost / memory of the run-away Stella as sexual narrative in and of herself: present in all sexual references:

> But all of a sudden, there she was, inside my head, Stella. Her smoky, spicy scent was so strong that, for a moment, I thought she really was there, upstairs, in our kitchen. I could even see her at the table with my mother, and me there, too, somehow, sitting between them, listening. (53)

It is the stubbornness and mystery of these women that moves Brenda: her hearing the suppressed narrative of childbirth as climax to sexuality that makes her feel she has made an enormous discovery. And it is a story that has to remain unacknowledged: a ghost story: Brenda cannot "let on" (54) that she has heard her mother's narrative of her own life's beginning inside her mother's body. Story: within story: within story. Sexual story so suppressed that it is reduced to a narrative of indirect blame: everything blamed on sexuality, but repressed so that in the actual narrative is a gap, an absence. Only when Brenda enters the ghostly narrative of sexual experience herself can she understand her own helplessness in the face of the taboo story.

The ghost story of sexual abuse is even more rigidly censored: haunted by anger: a narrative trapped in its own disbelief. Lee wants to announce: loudly: incontrovertibly: her fear of the dentist who abuses his position to fondle her: she wants to denounce him in a daily narrative voice the way her sister feels free to declare her physical need to urinate:

> "Dr. Allan's been feeling me up, every visit, for the last three years." I imagined saying this, out loud, in Lawson's, just after my mother had ordered the sundaes. "Feeling me up" was the perfect phrase. I imagined saying it in the clear, unembarrassed voice with which my sister Jill used to announce her need to pee. The voice of someone who doesn't give a sweet shit who's listening, someone who knows her rights. (133)

The fact that Lee never tells the story: never dares to tell the story: speaks to the essence of the ghost narrative at work. Her story would be questioned: wouldn't necessarily be believed. She cannot imagine articulating this scenario: and it is then that she knows what terrible danger she and her sister are in. The story that cannot be told is the story that holds us in thrall: that can do with us what it will. Without being able to narrate what is happening: censoring herself as she is censored by her parents, especially her father: she is powerless. Only when she gathers courage to infiltrate the master plan and refuse passivity: by sticking the dentist with one of his own tools: a dental pic: can she enter the narrative. Her action is its own accusation: and she only says: "You know" to the dentist when he asks her: "What in hell do you think you're trying to pull?" (137). He tries to take narrative control back from her by saying: "Just remember. No one's going to believe you… Who were you going to tell anyway, sweetheart?" (137): but he never touches her again: which can only mean that he has been forced to recognize her ghost presence in his deliberate strategy. She is no longer helpless.

Still, her story is a ghost story that continues to haunt her with its silence. She wants to tell her mother: her father: her sister: everything, but she never does: and in her reconstruction of the story, she mistrusts her memory: "Perhaps what I don't remember is worse, even, than what I do" (140). More important is Lee's mother's admission of the potential story in the letter she writes to Lee when Dr. Allan dies: "*I can't help thinking of you girls and that drill and no freezing*" (142). Her admission of the possible missing narrative is an offering: an apology for censorship and disbelief to the ghost narrative never permitted to be itself. So that the ghost of Lee's untold story is echoed by the ghost of her mother's inexplicit acknowledgement that there might have been an untold story: that danger did lurk in the official version.

Story Intuitive

In the same way does "Back Pain" try to decipher a ghost story: a story that can only be glanced at as emanation. A "Mother's Early Warning System" (89) for narrative disfunction: erasure: not quite present in the text: "Something is wrong. Something is wrong with Kate, but Barbara doesn't know what. Doesn't know what to ask, that is, or even if. And then what?" (93). How can event be plotted if it is not event? And even if the something wrong is admitted, its ghost is not so easily assuaged. Can what is absent here be reduced to plot and character? Who to trust here: the person? the life? the story? the instinct? or the ghostly emanation on the periphery of the surface narrative?

> Something is wrong. Something is very wrong for her daughter, Kate, and Barbara knows it. Knows it, but doesn't believe it.
> No. Scratch that. She believes it all right. She just doesn't know what to do about it. (99)

The story is: and then the story is: and then what? Which narrative can be trusted? Barbara's instinctive sense reads between the lines, recognizes the ghosts of fear and anxiety: Who can you trust? What can you be certain of if your daughter's boyfriend is battering her?

Only the story: Wallace tells us: only the story as it is peopled by the trust of the people you'd trust your life (story) to. "If This is Love" stories exactness as ghostly: open to doubt: "The history that matters is the history we can use" (55). "The hope of accuracy we bring to such tasks is crazy, heart-breaking"[6] Alice Munro says of our attempts to remember precisely: to inscribe our personal narratives with accuracy. Something always slips past us: inexplicable. Even prescriptions cannot save us from the ambush of surprise: the ghost story of "another country heard from" (60): ghost knowledge drifting into the narrative we have established as believable: the one we, perversely, want to test. How can Allison know what music her mother listened to while she was in the womb? And how can the limits of story: of body: of allergies or death be tested? Allison's allergies are her body's inscribement: an inner story, only intuited.

Story Braille

Memory may be hopeless, but it has the braille of fingers reading re-inscribement. In Wallace, there is always the possibility of the doubled narrative: the twice-written story: the re-lived life: re-marriage to a first love ("Heart of My Heart"): the repeated events of marriage, birth, death part of the master narrative, yes, but also their own shadow stories: idiosyncratic ghost spirits of the past invading the dominant narrative. Like scars rippling the surface of the skin, marring its textuality: the burn marks blooming around the waitress' wrists that Lydia ("Chicken 'n' Ribs") suddenly wants to kiss (25): the scars where Linda ("Heart of My Heart") has tried to cut her wrist, "covered with Band-Aids that had been stuck on any old way, dirty and puckered, so that beneath them I could see the masses of crude, ineffectual cuts and scabs" (9): the scar on the back of Gail's hand ("People You'd Trust Your life To") where her husband closed the door on her hand the first time he tried to get away (162): the scar where a prisoner ripped Roy ("For Puzzled in Wisconsin") open in in one swipe:

> Across his middle, from his belt line to just below his left nipple was a wide, jagged, white scar. He had a lot of hair, but it hadn't grown back over the scar, which was thicker in some places than others. It glistened and bulged in the yellow kitchen light, stretched taut over his gut as if the skin couldn't take much more. (82)

Scars speak their own mystery of what has been done to the whole and perfect skin of narrative: they speak interruption to the body's story, its capacity to accept inscribement. For Anna, Roy and his scar are a story that she likes to tell: and she tells it often: although it is only a part of the story of the summer when she worked as a waitress at a lodge in Muskoka.

Scars are also faint signposts to narrative and shadow stories of their own: perhaps stories that can only be read with braille: Wallace's especial braille of touch:

> what I can see now is a closeup of Joan's hand, reaching out to Roy's bare gut, caressing it so intimately I can't believe she's doing it in front of us. And then, with the tip of her index finger, gently, very gently, she traces the scar, every turn and bulge, from Roy's nipples to his waist, as if to show us exactly what it's like.
>
> As if his belly were a map, almost, and the scar was this road she was pointing out, wanting us to see where he'd been. And where she'd been too. (84)

The trust required of touch becomes an emblem of narrative and memory: touch its own ghost whispering past the guidelines of expectation.

Story Presence

But despite memory, Wallace knows the harbingers of recognition that ghosts bring to the stories that they haunt. Presence: its photographic presence, is recognizable. The teller in "The Scuba Diver in Repose" telling finally in her photographs the story of presence and the presence of absence. She claims that being a teller (telling money presumably; in a bank presumably): is her "real" work: that photography is "just a hobby" (168): but she is a teller / ghost for the photographer of the invisible. Her photographic attempts to capture presence (past obvious physical presence) as an absence enable her to evoke previously unknown (unwritten) recognitions.

The teller / narrator / photographer (Gillian Stewart) in this story tells a narrative of inverse death: the way that story can come to life and pay attention to itself, as she does (170): in the same way that it can refuse to recognize itself, as some of her photographic models do: "one of the women from work, Helen, was actually angry. My parents didn't even recognize themselves" (172). The teller has no special access to a bank of information, but forces us to recognize what we have never seen before: and her story is haunted by its own haunting. Diane Arbus' line, "It's what I've never seen before that I recognize" (176) becomes the teller / photographer's reprise: becomes the story's reprise: becomes the reader's reprise: the choric voice / ghost that points to presence previously unrecognized. Recognition becomes a haunting. The teller of the tale can photograph the impossible: the unseen: the story's ghost: "I began to see that very often people were most themselves when they didn't look it, when they were unrecognizable in all the usual ways" (171).

In seeing the document / story / photograph, we too become witness to the ghost presence: implicated in bank robbery: the bank the teller works in a hoarding of detail in photographs (representational images): detail that tells all that we do not know we know but that we recognize. Not plot: not characterization: but the instant of refusal, the person known as they are not known: as "other" to their usual story / representation. The obverse narrative: not simply unexpected but invented. Presence: knowledge that materializes in a developing tray.

And does the teller not determine how and where the narrative can die? When Jimmie (the scuba diver who dives beneath the surface: who can recognize what he's never seen: who insists on the teller / photographer learning to look: seeing what is not there but nevertheless present) dies, the ghost of his death becomes the presence that the photographer / teller does not want to record or recognize because once she does she will have to efface herself in order never to see it.

Again, the spaces in / between the story provide for the presence that is so absent to the grieving narrator: but also leave room for the breath of the story's ghost to breathe: along with the breath Gillian has been holding for a long, long time: until: until: until: at last, she can turn the narrative's face to the light: permit its angle of recognition. The beauty of this story resides very much in its hauntedness: the teller / photographer's inability to tell, and yet the inevitable necessity of recognition as telling. And in the end, the destroyed photographs (impossible to replicate in narrative) become the story's ghosts: absent and present: both extant and destroyed.

That "The Scuba Diver in Repose" completely undermines the notions of content and characterization that we clutch so determinedly is only a small part of the way that the narrative haunts itself. It is even more brilliant for its implicated but subversive employment of death as the traditional narrative ending. Along with the death of narrative's focus on death as a happy (sic) ending motive is the (narrativized) death of the character Jimmie: but even more complex and moving, the death of Wallace (extra-narratively) herself. It is as if she is writing from beyond the margin of death: as if her own dying haunts the presence of absence in these stories she wrote just before she died. At the same time, this presence utterly explodes the narrative convention / element of *denouement*. Truly, the reader / witness is haunted here by haunted story.

Story De / Railed

Expectation resists the story that is trying to tell itself, complete with ghosts. "That's what I'm tryin' to tell you, goddamnit!" (143) Gail declares at the beginning of "People You'd Trust Your Life To" and on the heels of her own declaration wonders about her son: "Maybe he's trying to tell me something and I'm too stupid to get it" (144). What story is the story trying to tell us? The four women of Good Girls Gobble and Gossip Group recount their stories to one another regularly: they behave reprehensibly: they talk volubly: they rail at one another. They become masters of each others' narratives, but never permit themselves to sink into a master narrative.

They worry about their children trying to change their life stories. They themselves have changed their own stories: Selena's three and a half incarnations: from Susie Patterson to Suzi to Suzi Sims to Selena Bluestone: re-writing herself to suit her own ghost narrative They have all, the four women, chosen their names and their colours to camouflage themselves: yet, they count on each other: they place their living narratives in one another's hands: they count on each other to read this slippery and deceptive story called life: to read between the lines.

Myrna imagines the four women as they might be read by the people next door: "how they must look…. All lit up like this, the stereo blaring…. Four middle-aged women sitting around a table full of dirty dishes in a kitchen that looks like it's been through a war, getting drunker than hell" (158). They are, these four women, in their narrative insurrection, going through one another's stories: infiltrating the narrative: the tension, and the setting, the climax and the denouement. They are destined to partake of one another's plot: to slip a word in here and there. They have engraved their mutual and distinct histories: they trust each other with their lives by trusting each other with their stories: the ghost narrations that save them. They traverse the countries of each others' futures: and they know the secrets and the hauntings of their inside lives. These are the people you can trust your life / story to: separate from the master narrative of judgement or expectation: the rigidities of protagonist / antagonist / witness. No divisions here, only the beautiful bones of narratives that have escaped the cages of their prisoners.

These are people you'd story your life to:

Stories you'd trust your people to:

People you'd trust your life (story) to:
And here it is.

Notes

1. All references to Bronwen Wallace's short story collection, *People You'd Trust Your Life To* (McClelland & Stewart, 2001) appear in the text in parentheses.
2. For a good time, see J. Hillis Miller on "Narrative" in *Critical Terms for Literary Study*, edited by Frank Lentricchia and Thomas McLaughlin, U of Chicago P, 1995, pp. 66-79. He has it all figured out: except for ghosts: and their indefinable essence.
3. J. Hillis Miller again, re-framing Aristotle, p. 69.
4. J. Hillis Miller reduces further, p. 75.
5. Linda Hutcheon, "Incredulity Toward Metanarrative: Negotiating Postmodernism and Feminisms." *Tessera*, vol. 7, Fall 1989, pp. 39-44.
6. Alice Munro. *Lives of Girls and Women*. Signet, 1974, p. 210.

Wanda Campbell
The Body as Map in the Work of Wallace

In what was to be her final public appearance, a keynote address entitled "Blueprints for a Larger Life" for International Women's Week in March 1989, Bronwen Wallace proposed using "our bodies as a guide to understanding why we are here today [....] Each of us then, by our physical presence, represents both possibility and limitation" (*AW* 215-216). In poems from each of her five collections of poetry, in the short stories in *People You'd Trust Your Life To*, and in the prose collected in *Arguments with the World*, Wallace finds ways within the context of the "particulars and politics of where we are" (*AW* 205) to pay attention to the body as both limitation and possibility. The phrase from Flannery O'Connor, "Possibility and limitation mean about the same thing," which Wallace chose as the epigraph for *The Stubborn Particulars of Grace*, is clarified by O'Connor with the following: "art transcends its limitations only by staying within them," (170) or, as Wallace put it in a letter to Erin Mouré, there is power in "the female understanding of the body as a limit we can love" (*Two Women Talking* 22). In the imagery of the body that permeates her work, Wallace explores the complex and shifting relationship between possibility and limitation. As literal and figurative manifestations of both, our vulnerable human bodies connect us with our past, our pain, and our planet, providing us with a map, to use another of Wallace's favourite tropes (47 *supra*), to guide us.

In *Figures of Dissent*, Terry Eagleton writes: "[t]he body, then, has been at once the focus for a vital deepening of radical politics, and a desperate displacement of them" (130). As David Hillman and Ulrika Maude point out in their Introduction to *The Cambridge Companion to The Body in Literature*, "the body is notoriously difficult to theorize or pin down, because it is mutable, in perpetual flux, different from day to day and resistant to conceptual definition" (1). Where once the body was seen as "a mere auxiliary to the self, a vehicle or object that houses the mind or the soul" to ultimately be shed like clothing, both scientists and philosophers are now suggesting that the body "participates in crucial ways in thinking, feeling and the shaping of our personalities and that precisely for this reason, the body is in fact constitutive of what we call the self" (1). As Wallace maintains in "Walkin' Shoes," "my spirit needs my lungs, needs the space they have to work in, which the body gives" (*KCBB* 15); we cannot do without the symbiotic relationship between who we are and the bodies that house us, however imperfectly.

The body has long been central to Wallace's understanding of her craft. In 1978, two years before her first collection of poetry was published, she drew attention to the pervasive presence of female bodies in the fiction of Alice Munro. "In Munro's development of character, we are never far from the persistent reality of their physical bodies. Women's bodies [...] are as much a definition of the characters as their thoughts, their beliefs and their interactions" ("Women's Lives" 56). Wallace situates her analysis in the context of Munro's apparent attempt to find a silver lining in a lack of power: "A subject race has a kind of clarity of vision and I feel that women have always had a clarity of vision which men were denied" ("Women's Lives" 56).

Elsewhere in this volume, Brenda Vellino explains the significance of the body:

> Wallace's longstanding experience in female and feminist communities such as Kingston's first stage Interval house for women and children at risk from domestic violence provides a context for her wider ethical engagement. Perhaps because women's social experience has been lived out through the legal, medical, economic, cultural, and domestic construction of their

bodies, "the body" and its inscription is central to any feminist theorizing. (96 *supra*)

There is certainly ample evidence of the body as limitation throughout Wallace's poetry and prose as a place of weakness, vulnerable to disease and destruction.

In her essay, "On Being Ill," that first appeared in T.S. Eliot's *The Criterion* in 1926, Virginia Woolf wrote:

Considering how common illness is, how tremendous the spiritual change that it brings, how astonishing, when the lights of health go down, the undiscovered countries that are then disclosed [...] it becomes strange indeed that illness has not taken its place with love, battle, and jealousy among the prime themes of literature. (193)

Woolf echoes Shakespeare's description in *Hamlet* of death as "the undiscovered country from whose bourn / no traveller returns" (III.i.80-81) and Wallace echoes Woolf in the "intricate countries" and "hidden lives" (*CM* 27) she seeks to reveal in poem after poem, story after story. Woolf continues:

literature does it best to maintain that its concern is with the mind; that the body is a sheet of plain glass through which the soul looks straight and clear and save for one of two passions such as desire and greed is null and negligible and non-existent. On the contrary, the very opposite is true. All day, all night the body intervenes; blunts or sharpens, colours or discolours ... the body smashes itself to smithereens, and the soul (it is said) escapes. But of all this daily drama of the body there is no record. (193-194)

When it comes to speaking of disease that is so much a part of the human experience, "there is nothing ready-made" (194), writes

Woolf. "Yet it is not only a new language that we need, more primitive, more sensual, more obscene, but a new hierarchy of the passions; love must be deposed in favour of a temperature of 104…" (195). Wallace was an admirer of Woolf, and in her poetry, she has responded to Woolf's invitation to forge a new language to wrestle with physical limitations and the mystery of mortality.

In the early poem "Heredity," from *Marrying into the Family*, the poet experiences an accident that involves "a simple operation" to restore her knee, so it is "as good as new" (*MF* 60). In contrast, the "smashed" kneecap of her grandmother "thrown from a buggy" requires a crutch for the rest of her life; bones are equally vulnerable to fracture then and now, but what has improved are the cures. Even in a broken state on the way to the Operating Room, the persona remembers the stories of this earlier knee, and those broken bones "knit themselves under [her] familiar skin" (60), with a verb that echoes one of the traditional modes of female making, thus providing a chain of story between the past and the present. The past, even in a damaged condition, can "knit" together the present through what is inherited along the lines of blood; the treasures of heredity are both tangible and intangible. In this early poem, Wallace gives us a rudimentary but relevant portrait of how the body demonstrates both limitation and possibility. In this poem, as Barbara Godard points out, "There's a sense of a bodily connection between women. Then it moves in the later book to be a discursive connection, a connection through language, in terms of social forces. This is the shift it has been suggested that must come about in order for political action of resistance to take place" (43).

The body's relationship to language is much more complex in "A Stubborn Grace" which is a four-part poem extending over seven pages of Wallace's second collection, *Signs of the Former Tenant*. In this case, the vulnerability and limitation are not the result of a single sudden accident, but the slow diminishment of disease. In a 1988 interview, Wallace explained that for five years, she was with a friend who was dying of Hodgkin's disease. "She was a very remarkable woman in that she was using her death as a way of teaching herself about how to lead her life. She taught me a lot about how I wanted to live my life" (Meyer 106).

The limitations of disease, that state of frailty to which all humans are subject in its most devastating form, are obvious. From the opening line of the poem, "The body chooses its own death" (*SFT* 103) through the many lines that follow, the poet learns, along with her dying friend, that death is not clean, or crisp, or ceremonial, but rather that it is cluttered, and complicated, and surprisingly conversational. Yes, there may be medication and pain, trembling fingers and a swollen abdomen, but the dying body with its bedsores and bruises is not the one the friends focus on but rather the "stubborn hands" that defy death through gestures of tenderness and grace. "The body chooses / and your hands attend the choice" (*SFT* 104). Stubbornly, hands continue on with their tasks of reaching for food, cradling a child, caring for a friend. Those who are still "so alive" wince in the face of mortality, but the dying one insists upon beauty and generosity and meaning. In "A Stubborn Grace," we hear an echo of Woolf in the poet's encounter with the "undiscovered country" on the other side of death: "your name is just another word / you've put aside for the ones / you are learning in the country of your dying" (*SFT* 107). As Wallace expresses it in the final lines in the final poem of *Signs of the Former Tenant*, the language of the body emerges at its most eloquent "when words are not enough / and the depth of what can't be said / reaches / to the bone" (*SFT* 109).

Literature, argue Hillman and Maude, "might in fact be understood as *the* place par excellence for the body to express itself, for an engagement with the problem of the relation between language and the body and for interrogating the enigma of embodied consciousness" (3). Bodies may not endure but the lessons they teach certainly do. After her friend's funeral, Wallace reflected on how all those she encountered were going to die:

> all of them are living in this state of frailty. They were all trying to figure out the mystery of their lives as much as I was trying to figure out the mystery of my own life. That's what death gives to us, the chance to do that [...] that recognition allows me to look at the people with a certain ... love, I guess. (Meyer 107)

In her explorations of the limitation and possibility of the body, Wallace reminds us that we face death "totally alone" and "inextricably connected" (Meyer 107).

Perhaps no part of human anatomy is more evocative of this dichotomy than the hand which, in her review of the French translation of Wallace's poems, Élise Lepage calls the "synecdoche of action" (73). In her correspondence with Erin Mouré, Wallace explains, "I write the way I do because [...] everything I have learned of value, I have learned from or through women and because I believe that gentleness is in the hands, regardless of gender" (*Two Women Talking* 36). Hands, and the loving gestures they make, figure largely in "A Stubborn Grace" but assume even more prominence in the poem "Learning from the Hands" from *Common Magic* because they so perfectly epitomize the limitation and possibility suggested by the body as a whole. The poem opens with the assertion that the evolutionary progress humans have made within the animal kingdom is mostly due to our hands, our fingers and opposable thumbs that have led to our capacity to realize and record our own feats of creation. Writes Eagleton:

> What is special about the human body, then, is just its capacity to transform itself in the process of transforming the material bodies which surround it [....] The human body is that which is able to make something of what makes it; and in this sense its

paradigm is language, a given which continually generates the unpredictable. (131-32).

"Some hands can see," argues Wallace (*CM* 85), going on to provide a list of examples as evidence of the spectacular power of hands, beginning with the hands of the blind where the ability to "see" braille is a kind of synesthetic tour de force. Perhaps less obvious are the hands of "certain healers" and of potters, wood-carvers and pregnant mothers, all of whom can discern what lies within through the magic of touch.

In the third stanza, Wallace reveals how vulnerable we are to the hands of others, how we trust our lives to the hands of doctors, carpenters, engineers, "some guy tightening bolts on an assembly-line somewhere" (*CM* 86). We have no choice, she seems to say, from the moment of our birth, but to deliver ourselves into the hands of others, trusting in the magic hands of those who fix the machines we depend upon and fix the bodies that we wear. Hands, however, like the rest of the natural world, can be manipulated. The limitations of those who can control the hands can become our own. "This is how we live, / in a world run by thugs / who think a hand is just a weapon / like the body / a machine for following orders" (*CM* 86). Wallace draws attention to how hands with all their sensitive nerve-ends can become sites both of torture and fortune telling where our own deaths can be foretold through the "palm's cartography" (*CM* 87); "how often they must measure / the little they can do / against how long it takes" (*CM* 86).

In the final stanza Wallace returns once again to the possibilities of hands as tools of repair and restoration, of craft and creation: "they are the needles thought needs to piece / the world together" (*CM* 87). To those intent on limitation, hands may be "just a weapon" but to those who believe in possibility, "hands are the only arrows / of desire that can reach what they want, / [...] what we have instead of wings / the closest we can come to flight" (*CM* 87). As Eagleton puts it, "the fact remains that the human body is indeed a material object, and that this is an essential component of anything more creative we get up to. [...] The body which lays me open to exploitation is also the ground of all possible communication" (132).

The body as a site of exploitation is more fully explored in "Thinking with the Heart" also from *Common Magic*, which reflects Wallace's work at Interval House, a battered women's shelter. "That job / that wrenched me round" ("Bones" *SPG* 81) revealed to Wallace "that there isn't an 'us' and 'them' situation, that as women we are all in danger and that recognition of that changes not only how I look at the issue but how I look at myself, or how I look at where I am in this society. And it changes what I can do about it" (49 *supra*). The poem's first epigraph is drawn from photographer Diane Arbus, famous for her pictures of unconventional individuals. "*I work from awkwardness. By that I mean I don't like to arrange things. If I stand in front of something, instead of arranging it, I arrange myself*" (*CM* 59). The title, however, is drawn from the second epigraph, the policeman who says, "*The problem with you women is, you think with your heart*" (*CM* 59). His position becomes clear as the poem unfolds. The battered women he deals with refuse to charge their abusers, or change their minds once they have, because for them it is not so simple. Even if she gets him out of her bed, and her house and her life, he is still there in her head, in her children, under her skin. "... the man who beats her / is also the man she loves" (*CM* 60). The policeman erroneously believes that he is above such vulnerability, such fragility. "He thinks he thinks with his brain / as if it was safe up there / in its helmet of bone / away from all that messy business / of his stomach or his lungs" (*CM* 61). But to think this way, the poet argues, is to lose oneself. "Whatever it is you need / is what you must let go of now / to enter your own body" (*CM* 62). The poem that begins "the body is a limit / I must learn to love" (*CM*

59) ends with whatever you hear crying through your own four rooms which you must name "before you can love anything at all" (*CM* 62). The four chambers of the heart, Wallace seems to be saying, are the only rooms we can truly call our own. "When you get in touch with your damage, recognize and care for it, you also discover the source of your power" (*AW* 210). To recognize limitation is to invite possibility.

By the time we arrive at the poem "Bones" in her penultimate collection *The Stubborn Particulars of Grace* (1987), the last to be published while she was alive, bones have undergone a kind of metamorphosis from an ossuary of heritage to an unexpected but powerful armour. But here it is not the bone itself, but the eight-inch stainless steel pin from her mother's thigh that the woman taxi-driver counts on for protection. The poet imagines how "the doctor must have delivered the thing" (*SPG* 80) with all the visceral details of fat and muscle, as improbable she writes as "the foetus / pickled in a jar" (*SPG* 80). This leads her to reflect on her work at the crisis centre and the confessions she heard and couldn't stop talking about, as her interlocuter actively re-enters "the country of her own damage / from a new direction" (*SPG* 81). "This," the poet says, leaving the antecedent ambiguous, "can be like watching someone we love / return from the limits a body can be taken to / —a botched suicide, say, or an accident" (*SPG* 81). She then reflects on all the years it takes for the mind, like the body, to offer a sign that it is regaining itself. Meanwhile the bones are showing up in the X-rays as light, "a translucence that belies their strength / or renders it immeasurable, / like the distance we count on them to carry us, / right to the ends of our lives and back again, / and again" (*SPG* 82). Possibility and limitation do indeed, as O'Connor contends, mean about the same thing.

"Bodily Fluids," like all but one of the poems in Wallace's final poetry collection *Keep That Candle Burning Bright* (1991), is a prose poem. "Wallace's relational subject," argues Vellino, "finds a formal analogue in her hybrid lyric form, which weaves literary, visual, musical and documentary media together to break down hierarchical categories of elite and popular culture" (97 *supra*). Wallace's engagement with the body that began with structured and skeletal connections between past and present, has become much more fluid in form and content, sliding easily between what Vellino calls "a porous weave of discourses" (97 *supra*). Though we have moved from firm bones to flowing fluids, the body remains central to this posthumously published collection from the epigraph taken from W.S. Merwin's poem "When You Go Away": "My words are the garment of what I shall never be / Like the tucked sleeve of a one-armed boy" to the final poem "Miracles" which suggests that the divine does still intervene in the daily.

"Bodily Fluids" appears in the section called "Everyday Science" which Wallace described as a series based on "scientific" material found in the tabloids. Working from the theory "that the way we think is directly related to the brain's being 80% water" (*KCBB* 45), the poet ponders how easily bodily fluids can be transferred, like giving blood for the Red Cross at the Legion hall, and how you have no idea where the blood may end up, so the poet's may end up in a conservative banker, while that of the man beside her might end up in a radical feminist. She goes on to reflect on how enough semen is ejaculated annually in England and Wales to fill one and half Olympic size swimming pools (*KCBB* 46). Another man also giving up his blood, draws her attention to two articles, one about loneliness killing more people than cigarettes, reminding her of whales beaching themselves, and the other with a headline about surgeons discovering that sea coral is the best substitute for human face bones.

This final image brings us full circle to the notion that our bodies tie us in ways we are just beginning to understand to the planet on which we live. As Vellino points out, Wallace's "practice of an ecological poetics is most manifest in her body imagery, which persistently reminds us of the material, biological and chemical elements that we share with human and more-than-human others" (104 *supra*). We are all connected, and we sever that connection at our peril. Not long before cancer took her life at the age of 44, Wallace said: "There's so much power in the body. If we would learn to attend to the power, we would learn not to fear what our bodies do. It's connected to how we see the body of the earth; by denying that we're part of the body of the earth, we're going to kill it" (*AW* 208).

The body as a map of what it means to be human through limitation and possibility also permeates Wallace's short fiction. As Smaro Kamboureli argues in "The Body as Audience and Performance in the Writing of Alice Munro,"

> Canadian women writers, whether they adhere to a radical or non-radical feminist ideology, or whether they choose forms and structures that conform to the literary tradition or depart from it, they all take exception to the anemic double of the feminine body that male language and mythology have constructed. They do so by deconstructing the culture that has hosted them as parasites. (31-32)

In the first three stories in *People You'd Trust Your Life To*, the body is presented as both limitation and possibility. In "Heart of My Heart," Linda's wrists with their "masses of crude, ineffectual cuts and scabs" (9) as evidence of her battle with her own mortality are contrasted with Mike's "fine, almost womanly" hands "picking things up, straightening, rearranging" (13) as he wills her to stay alive the way his first wife did not. In "Chicken 'n' Ribs," Lydia's "*forgotten*" hand that looks at once like a child's and an old woman's is contrasted to the hand of her waitress dotted with burn marks she wants to kiss. "She wants to hold that hand between her two and rub it as she used to rub the pain from her children's fingers when they played outside too long in the snow…" (25). In "Fashion Accents," the mother's no-nonsense routine of "half squat to splash her armpits, breasts and crotch" (41) and the "ripe, sweetish smell" her body exudes like "vegetables that had been in the fridge too long" is contrasted with the "swollen and zingy" way her daughter's young body feels "as if [her] blood were pushing against [her] skin in all the places Fraser had touched [her], making them incandescent…" (51). Limitation and possibility shine through these stories and the bodies they contain.

In the next three stories, bodies figure even more prominently, almost as entities with a will of their own beyond the control of those who inhabit them. In "If This is Love," killer allergies manifest as rashes and welts, "pure malevolence, wilful and implacable" (66) on the skin of young Allison, the child who holds her parents together even after divorce with a physicality that "rejects all their fine plans, in fact, as fiercely as the body rejects our attempts to make it more or less than simply what it is" (70). In "For Puzzled in Wisconsin," the body is "a map, almost" (84) with scars as roads that show us where its owner has been, to such a degree that a woman in Wisconsin wonders if she can keep the intricate tattoo on her husband's chest after he has died, and the narrator Anna wonders what her husband might wish to keep of her as a souvenir, "some of my stretch marks? The mole on my left breast?" (79). Roy, the former guard at the Kingston Pen who is sliced open with a shank, bears a "wide, jagged, white scar" stretching from his nipple to waist (82), but rather than finding it repulsive, his wife Joan caresses it as part of what makes him who he is, a map of where he's been and where he's headed.

Again, in "Back Pain," physical pain and psychological or "spiritual pain" are conflated, and Bev, the masseuse, espouses a "hippy-dippy theory about how all the pain you've ever experienced (since childhood, for godsake) is trapped inside your body until you decide to work it out" (86). No matter how many times Bev tells Barbara "*Let go of this pain*" (85), Barbara remains unconvinced, and yet she herself diagnoses the health of her own children by their hair, as part of what her husband calls MEWS, "Mother's Early Warning System" (89). And it is, indeed, her daughter's "lank and stringy" hair (88) that reveals to Barbara that all is not well with the new boyfriend Danny, no matter how charming he appears. Lines from a 1637 poem by Sir John Suckling vaguely remembered from high school "*Why so pale and wan fond lover? Prithee why so pale?*" (88) surface in Barbara's mind as a reminder of the perils of unrequited love. She turns out to be right, and the invisible psychological pain the boyfriend has been inflicting on her daughter ultimately makes its way out to the visible pain of bruises and a black eye.

In "An Easy Life," whether you have an easy life with educational and socio-economic opportunities like Marion or you don't like Tracey, in the end one's body decides one's future. "Marion's own death ticks in her cells as it does in anybody's. Anything can happen, any time" (117). In "Tip of My Tongue" death and decay find their way into the body, like the tapeworm the father so horrifyingly describes, the gum diseases, or the repeated molestation of the dentist when the narrator was a girl. Stancy, like the "hippy dippy" Bev of the earlier story, believes one can use pain "as a guide" (131) to what is really wrong with us. The father forbids anaesthetic at the dentist, coffee or canned food, and warm clothing because "tough bodies build tough characters" (126), but he does not realize that the bodies of his own daughters are in danger.

In "People You'd Trust Your Life To," scars are again a guide to what people have been through, "landmark[s] in a familiar country" (144), like the many stitches sported by Suzi's sons who are "veterans of an endless and increasingly alarming conflict between the human body and various pieces of sports equipment"

(150) or, far more disturbingly, the cigarette burns on Gail's son's small behind, or the scar on Gail's hand from the time her husband closed the door on it when she tried to get away.

In "The Scuba Diver in Repose," the final story in the first edition of *People You'd Trust Your Life To* (1990), the metaphor for paying attention to the body as map is photography. Photographs are what tie the narrator to the scuba diver she loves, and what she must destroy if she is to get past his death. "You have to learn how to use your eyes all over again" (169) he says of the underwater worlds he explores, and this is also true of the photographs she learns to take with his encouragement, photos of people who "were most themselves when they didn't look it" (171), and of the world of death that he passes into, leaving her behind. Wallace quotes Diane Arbus twice in the story, first when he is dying, "It's what I've never seen before that I recognize" (176), and after he's gone and his parents send her a photo of him as a small boy blowing out birthday candles (185). In Wallace's fiction as in her poetry, "The body chooses its own death" (*SFT* 103.)

In her article on "The Scuba Diver in Repose," Janice Kulyk Keefer traces an evocative comparison with Roland Barthes' *Camera Lucida* which is relevant to our current discussion since Barthes describes photography as a medium that affects the body as much as the mind. Kulyk Keefer quotes Barthes at length:

> The photograph is literally an emanation of the referent. From a real body, which was there, proceed radiations which ultimately touch me, who am here. The duration of the transmission is insignificant; the photograph of the missing being, as Sontag says, will touch me like the delayed rays of a star. A sort of umbilical cord links the body of the photographed thing to my gaze: light, though impalpable, is here a carnal medium, a skin I share with anyone who has been photographed. (224)

Barthes' *Camera Lucida* has been read as a eulogy to his late mother and a harbinger of his own imminent death, and Kulyk Keefer speaks eloquently of the way Wallace's story echoes our own sense of loss: "For this story, which deals so movingly with a woman grieving over her lover's death, expresses my own grief at its author's dying, as well as that author's own farewell to her art, to her life, to the vision she related so stubbornly and with such integrity to the vulnerable, resilient, perishable human body" (225).

When a new edition of *People You'd Trust Your Life To* was published in 2001, an additional story first published in *Descant* in 1992 was included, and it is hard not to view "Lillian on the Inside" as a kind of valediction, in that the titular character bequeaths small parting gifts to each of her children. With the exception of the five one hundred dollar bills she leaves to Karen, the daughter she almost chose not to have, all of her "gifts" are somehow related to the body. For Ellen, her oldest who was "her extra pair of hands" (198), Lillian leaves a xerox of her own hands. Ellen, we discover, disappeared at sixteen for seven years, a time frame in which "every cell in your body renews itself," repeating "everything that had already happened to you, birthmarks, scars and all" as well as "all the new stuff too" (199). For her son Mike who was "pure boy [...] no part of his body was without cut or scrapes, scars, bruises, casts or splinters" (201), she leaves a postcard of Houdini hanging upside down with the advice, "never stop planning your escape" (203). For her daughter Lisa who loves a woman and fills her home with little surprises from the natural world, she leaves a feather from the body of a bird. And then to her youngest son Carl, a photograph of the whole family with Carl running into a patch of sunlight "as if he is (disintegrating?") into pure air" (211).

She also leaves words of gratitude for her husband Art (surely not an accidental choice of name): "From our two bodies we have made our love and our children and our life [...] Because of our bodies you know things about me no one else does and because of you I know things about myself I couldn't know any other way" (205). Art is intimately aware of the silvery stretch marks that make "her body into a map, so that every time she needs to see her life" (204) she has only to look down. On the way to mail her final letters, Lillian meets a girl holding colourful balloons trying to escape, and the two look at one another with "the same expressions of sorrow and amazement" (213), bringing the reader full circle to limitation and possibility once more.

To end where we began, in "Blueprints for a Larger Life," Wallace's final speech, she takes her discussion of bodies, the bodies of women in particular, into the realm of reality where they also demonstrate both limitation and possibility. On the one hand, women's bodies are beaten, raped, and exploited through prostitution and pornography. "There are women in every country whose bodies are worn out, twisted, maimed and diseased because of the work they must do" (*AW* 217). Bodies are starved and subjugated and silenced, and yet they still manage to speak out and make their presence known. As she does in several of her stories, Wallace draws attention to the fact that "body language" is often a clue to abuse, "stronger even than the conscious mind" (*AW* 217). In reality, as in Wallace's poetry and fiction, the body serves as a map and guide and early warning system, both to what is happening to it and to the planet. Wallace argues that attempts to exert control over the human body are connected to "continued attempts to exert control over the bodies of other animals, and ultimately over the body of the earth" (*AW* 224) since as she puts it in her poem "Daily News," "we're only another species after all" (*CM* 35). Yet on the possibility side of the ledger, there is no denying "the hard, stubborn fact that life depends on women's bodies" (*AW* 220). According to Hillman and Maude:

> In confronting us with the legible materiality of the body, literature often provides powerful forms of resistance to socially instituted perceptions and demands. [...] Authorities (medical and socio-economic and political) have powerfully vested interest in constructing bodies in particular ways; literature, throughout the ages, works to remind us of this fact and thereby to deconstruct these myths often by reinstating the delirium and the scandalousness of the body. (5)

By exploring the unpredictable limitations and possibilities of bodies, especially female bodies, and how they resist definition and fixity at every turn, Wallace manages to contest the stereotypes and hierarchies of our culture. She challenges us to replace "power over, which is the only kind of power this culture understands" (*AW* 220) with the "power to" that comes from within and enables action. As Vellino puts it, "From deep attention to the vulnerable body, which humans share with others grows Wallace's ethical engagement with the body's world" (96 *supra*). For Wallace, our approach to the body reflects our priorities. "We focus on replacing parts of the body with new organs, as if it was a machine, and talk very little about living a life that would protect that body we've already got" (*AW* 74).

Throughout her oeuvre, the body serves as a map of our past, our pain, and our planet, and the potential of all three to remind us what it means to be human. In the world Wallace has created for us, the body is the most reliable indicator of our limitation and our possibility and the only language we have left when words fail. "News of the Dead," the penultimate poem in *Keep That Candle Burning Bright*, is a reflection on the departed in the tabloids where people never really die, but keep on giving interviews and advice, keep on appearing in unlikely places. "The residue from their bodies will continue shining from our windows at night..." (*KCBB* 51-52), and so it is that three decades after her own death, Bronwen's words still burn bright.

Works Cited

Eagleton, Terry. *Figures of Dissent*. Verso, 2003.

Godard, Barbara with Mary di Michele. "'Patterns of Their Own Particular Ceremonies': A Conversation in an Elegiac Mode, between Mary di Michele and Barbara Godard." *Open Letter*, vol. 7, no. 9, 1991, pp. 36-59.

Hillman, David and Ulrika Maude. *The Cambridge Companion to the Body in Literature*. Cambridge UP, 2015.

Kamboureli, Smaro. "The Body as Audience and Performance in the Writing of Alice Munro." *Amazing Space: Writing Canadian, Women Writing*. Longspoon/Newest, 1986, pp 31-38.

Kulyk Keefer, Janice, "'Telling Our Grief': Photographic Image in Bronwen Wallace's 'The Scuba Diver in Repose'" *Image et Récit: Littérature(s) et Arts Visuels du Canada*. Presse Sorbonne Nouvelle, 1993, pp. 209-227.

Lepage, Élise. "Poésie." *University of Toronto Quarterly*, vol. 87, no. 3, 2018, pp. 64-84.

Meyer, Bruce and Brian O'Riordan. "The Telling of Stories: An Interview with Bronwen Wallace." *Lives & Works: Interviews by Bruce Meyer and Brian O'Riordan*. Black Moss, 1992, pp.100-107.

O'Connor, Flannery. *Mystery and Manners: Occasional Prose*. Farrar, Straus & Giroux, 1979.

Wallace, Bronwen. "Women's Lives: Alice Munro." *The Human Elements: Critical Essays* edited by David Helwig. Oberon, 1978, pp. 52-67.

---. *Two Women Talking: Correspondence 1985 to 1987 Erin Mouré and Bronwen Wallace*. Living Archives of The Feminist Caucus of the League of Canadian Poets, 1993.

Woolf, Virginia, "On Being Ill." 1926. *Collected Essays*. Hogarth, 1967, vol. 4, pp. 193-203.

Phyllis Webb
Bronwen's Earrings

long, or large and circular
the only decoration on her
tall frame, her plain façade
the better to hear the high
vibrations of your health, your
sorrows. A touch of fantastic
as she moved her head
to follow the plot
silver or gold flashing
hilarious light on the lure
of the pierced ear.
Spangles. Trapezoids, fluttery
things. Wild bird.

The pair I gave her
turquoise, oval, Chinese
I think and very long
with a history of survival.

As I drink this tea
on an ordinary day
someone crosses
a street in Kingston
picking up flute notes
soprano complaints
her earlobes tugged
by a small weight
of chimes
the need to be heard, desire.

Andrea Beverley
Reading Women Talking:
Feminist Poetics and the Bronwen Wallace –
Erin Mouré Correspondence

The list of course texts for my 2019 seminar on Canadian women writers included two very similar titles, *Women Talking* and *Two Women Talking*. The titles of both Miriam Toews' 2018 bestselling novel and Erín Moure and Bronwen Wallace's 1993 published correspondence use the same grammatical formulation to suggest not an adjective-subject phrase (talking women) but an active, collaborative activity ("women talking"). Listed together on the syllabus, the titles' notable similarity was striking and begged the question, what is it about women talking? In Toews' novel, the women talking are from generations of two families, covertly gathered in a hayloft to debate whether or not they should abscond from their secluded, dangerous Mennonite colony. Their conversation is high stakes, wide-ranging, and textualized by a minute-taking narrator. In Moure and Wallace's text, the "talking" is actually writing, though the epistolary back-and-forth does evoke a conversational mode. Further, the understanding of poetics that Wallace articulates throughout the correspondence repeatedly centres women talking, women's voices, conversations, and stories. Her poem "Bones," her essay "One More Woman Talking," and a series of "readings, meditations" within the correspondence describe Wallace's vision of feminist poetry-making in terms corroborated in her larger oeuvre. Themselves texts that prioritize conversation, the trio of "Bones," "One More Woman Talking," and the "readings, meditations" can be read in conversation with each other and with their intertexts within and beyond Wallace's oeuvre, including those that emerge in a classroom context.

Wallace's poem "Bones" (*SPG* 80) begins with a dedication, "*for Barb*," and then: "A story of yours got this one going." For the poetic speaker, and for Wallace writing, conversation between women sparks poetic creation. Stories inspire, render possible, and sustain the explorations and musings that comprise the poetry.[1] The poem continues, "so I'm sending it back now, changed, of course," signaling that the story is inevitably transformed by this particular poetic iteration. Though the story has been offered and "sent back," the exchange is immediately compared not with a transaction, but with the experience of the speaker calibrating herself in the presence of her loved ones: "I'm sending it back now, changed, of course, / just as each person I love / is a re-location, where I take up / a different place in the world" (*SPG* 80). These lines emphasize the individuality of every loving relationship, distinctions so particular that with each loved one, the speaker feels like she occupies a different geographical location. The metaphorical equation between beloveds and locations comes up elsewhere in Wallace's poetry as well: speakers conjure "all my other loves, locate each one / precisely, as I could this house / on a city map" ("Particulars" *SPG* 111) or proclaim "some people are a country / and their deaths displace you" ("Coming Through" *CM* 33).[2] The simile-making "just as" in the third line of "Bones" means that the poetic process that *begins in* relationship, in talking and listening, is also *compared to* relationship, to the different positions one occupies vis-à-vis a beloved other. The latter circles back to the former because it is in those relational positions, in conversation, that stories are told. The love and the story make change for the speaker: they are impactful and generative.

In its evocation of women's stories, parental figures, bodies sick and threatened and recovering, great vulnerability and great strength, "Bones" is a poem typical of Wallace's oeuvre. Following the first five lines discussed above, the poem recounts Barb's story of a woman taxi driver who keeps a steel shank extracted from her mother's thigh under her car seat as a potential weapon. The speaker imagines how the shank could have gone from the surgeon to the daughter, and how its protective power conjures the mother's face "in the hall light, rescuing you / from a nightmare" (*SPG* 81). From there the speaker moves to the stories she offered back to Barb, stories of working in a crisis centre. The active listening with which one friend attends to the story of the other means that the listener revisits "her own damage / from a new direction" (*SPG* 81), an experience that is like watching a loved one come back from near death. The final image of the poem is of the titular "bones" as seen on an x-ray. There the bones "show up / as light, a translucence that belies their strength / or renders it immeasurable" (*SPG* 82).

In 1987, Wallace chose "Bones" as the poem that could stand in for a longer prose statement of her poetics. Scheduled to present at a League of Canadian Poets Feminist Caucus workshop on Women and Language, Wallace contributed "Bones" to the session handout and chapbook even though she had originally prepared a prose piece for the workshop (McMaster 83, 91; Ford and McMaster 41-42). Erín Moure was the primary organizer of the workshop so Wallace sent her poem to Moure in the context of their on-going correspondence. That same year, "Bones" was published in Wallace's *The Stubborn Particulars of Grace* as the final poem in the "Bones" sub-section. When Wallace and Mouré's 1985-1987 correspondence was published in 1993, "Bones" appeared therein as well, appended to her essay "One More Woman Talking." In describing the basis for her poems in "One More Woman Talking" Wallace explains, "I begin with what I have been given: women's stories, women's conversations. [...] [F]or me, that everyday language is a sort of safety net, a familiar place in which a deeper, often more dangerous exploration can take place" (38 *supra*). "Bones" serves as an enactment of that methodology.

The Mouré-Wallace letters were published as *Two Women Talking: Correspondence 1985-87*, edited by Susan McMaster, in the LCP Feminist Caucus's Living Archives series. The Feminist Caucus was founded within the League in 1982. The Living Archives series now includes nearly thirty titles, almost all of which capture material presented at the Caucus's annual meetings. Because it is not a proceedings, *Two Women Talking* is an exception: it is a collection of twenty letters that precede the Feminist Caucus workshop that sparked their conversation. The topic of the workshop, which Moure initially summarized as "aspect[s] of feminine voice, language, etc." (McMaster 15), gets them "talking" about their often divergent understandings of the connection between women and language. Moure writes effusively about the feminist potentials of deconstructive language poetics while Wallace passionately affirms feminists' capacity to write subversively within language.

Two Women Talking is a layered, polyvocal text, rich in intertextuality, and complexified by the fact that Moure was involved in its editing whereas Wallace died years before its publication. In one of the only critical engagements with the book, Patrick Finn analyses how the correspondence is mediated through its editorial framing, from Susan McMaster's "Note to the Reader" and Moure's "Foreword," to explanatory notes and excisions from the letters (Finn 104-106, 108, 111). Finn asks how the book's construction advantages or disadvantages each writer (108-109, 112). These important analytical questions emerge from the content and form of the book, features which prompt readerly curiosity about what really happened and who comes out stronger in the exchange. The epistolary format amplifies the debate-like qualities of Moure and Wallace's conversation, placing readers in the somewhat uncomfortable position of witnessing their tensions and feeling pressured to choose a side. This intriguing sense of voyeurism and discomfort has been palpable in classrooms when teaching this text. Although this exchange is between poets and about poetry, the general scenario may feel familiar: two feminist friends engage in a passionate exchange—sometimes disagreement—about patriarchy and women's liberation strategies. They express hurt and anger when they feel they are being misunderstood or dismissed (34, 37, 69). Toward the end of the correspondence, Wallace asks pointedly and poignantly, "Why do I feel that discussing women and language has, instead of drawing us closer, brought us to a landscape of strangeness and distance? Or am I the only one who feels this? This is an adult talking. Like the little girl—or the adolescent who would have said much more succinctly, 'Are you still my friend?'" (69).

Despite Moure's assurances in the Foreword that the end of the discussion was "perfectly amicable, and accompanied by an acceptance of the necessity of our parallel paths" (10), their shifting interpersonal dynamics are among the most engrossing aspects of the correspondence.[3] In class, students are intrigued by the friendship drama, clearly tempted to align themselves with one poet or the other. Who do they think is *right* about the relationship between gender and language? With whom do they most identify? One student observed, "I feel more sympathetic to Wallace but I realized that I'm more of a Moure." In the seminar, I wondered if I should pull our discussion away from this antagonistic reading, which pits the two writers against each other and felt somehow a little gossipy. The back-and-forth volley of their conversation, and the fact that they are indeed defending somewhat contradictory stances, made it easy for us to minimize them into caricatures of their standpoints. We began to say "Wallace" as shorthand for "believes in storytelling" and "easier to understand"; we said "Moure" and meant "theoretically edgier" and "suspicious of language." The temptation was to collapse their nuanced, careful, brilliant prose into inaccuracies.

Although some aspects of the content and form of this book elicit the side-taking I describe above, Wallace's own stance on the power of women's conversations calls us to a more generative interaction with this epistolary "conversation." Ultimately, in Finn's assessment, Wallace's voice "reaches out to us through the gaps, new and old: even when aspects of the editing could potentially operate to quiet her voice, she is heard loudly, clearly, and passionately telling her stories" (113). Here Finn uses the touchstones of Wallace's own poetics—gaps, voice, stories—to describe her presence among the pages. While "Bones" emphasizes stories and everyday voices as starting points for poetic exploration, one of her other pieces in *Two Women Talking* focuses more on the concept of gaps. In an April 1986 letter, Wallace offers what she calls "a departure, a lateral leap, from my former approach to the questions we have been discussing about language and writing" (49). Rather than explain her responses to various theoretical suppositions, she seeks to demonstrate how she sees the world through four "readings, meditations, if you will, on items which have power for me" (49). Her subsequent reflections on four very different objects, textual and otherwise, all take up the idea of gaps. More precisely, she refers to "chinks," conjuring cracks that let in light.

Throughout *Two Women Talking*, Wallace remains committed to the idea that there are potential chinks in monolithic, patriarchal systems. These fissures allow feminist analyses of the behind-the-scenes of sexist structures, or feminist readings that go against the grain of dominant misogynistic mainstream understandings. She objects to the feminist language theory that Moure shares with her in large part because she feels that it denies the possibility of such gaps in language, as if language itself were an unyielding, anti-woman system. Whether or not this is a misreading of Moure and the authors she quotes, Wallace clearly baulks at the idea of language as inherently problematic. Since stories, conversation, and everyday language are transformative and catalyzing in Wallace's poetics, she maintains that any critiques of language must nonetheless admit gaps that allow for women's voices. This is why her four April 1986 "readings, meditations" all recognize the overwhelming influence of "the ideology of a white, bourgeois, western, capitalist, patriarchal world view" *while also* arguing that there is always "a chink in the wall of determinism" (50, 51).

The four "readings, meditations" demonstrate the reading methodology through which she locates the gaps that also connect to her writing methodology. The first demonstration of this is "Part I: Wake Up and Smell the Coffee," in which Wallace "reads" her morning coffee. She begins by acknowledging that the cultural practices of breakfast and coffee, of taking her mug for granted, of particular associations with coffee, are all culturally determined. She then inserts a single-word sentence on its own line: "But." From there she describes what she learned about food production from her locavore father and what she learned about material and social relations under capitalism from reading Karl Marx and working with labour activists (50). These cumulative moments of consciousness raising allow her to see her coffee in relation to an imagined woman worker picking coffee beans whose life might be shaped by poverty, unjust working conditions, land theft, and violence (51). This woman is perceptible "through the chink."[4] As in many of Wallace's poems, an object—in this case the coffee mug—is a catalyst or metonymy for a broader point. In *Marrying into the Family*, domestic objects are connectors between people through storytelling, sale, heredity, or marriage (see, for instance, "Marriages," "Connecting," "Getting Down To It" and "Country Auction Sale"). Already prominent in her first collection, this feature of her poetry persists, culminating perhaps in *The Stubborn Particulars of Grace*'s "Things," in which the speaker states "it's things that connect us" (96). "Things" even features a coffee mug: "that coffee mug / you hold each morning / without even thinking of it / is a mystery" (97). In the case of "Part I: Wake Up and Smell the Coffee," the mug combines with life learnings to allow a vision of transnational solidarity. The section ends with a direct reference to Wallace's poetry, a striking conclusion to a piece that has not once mentioned her poetic practice. She asserts that in the freedom from determinism lies "the voice, which is mine alone, from which, on a good day, the true poems come" (51).

In the next two sections of this "readings, mediations" letter-essay, Wallace continues to demonstrate the methodology she used with the coffee mug. She provides against-the-grain readings of two texts, one a Brothers Grimm version of Cinderella and the other a woodcut of a Renaissance-era Caesarean section birth. In each case, Wallace offers feminist commentary that belies mainstream understandings of the stories. For instance, in her interpretation of Cinderella, Wallace highlights the crucial role of Cinderella's dead birth mother. In this version of the tale, the dead mother's spirit is incarnate in the animals and fairy godmother who help Cinderella. Her interventions are salvific and for Wallace, "it is the power of the mother which [...] gleams like an ancient light at the deepest level of this story" (55), a point she also makes about Cinderella in her essay "An Auction at Mother's Childhood Home" (*AW* 151). She does not ignore the dominant readings of Disneyesque Cinderella ("of course the Prince is a problem"—54) but her focus is a feminist recuperation of the maternal power that drives the plot. For her, this is an example of "another chink in the wall, a gap in the patriarchal language, through which another voice speaks, another power recreates its existence" (55). Strikingly, she uses the word "power" over a dozen times in this two and half page text.

In her reflection on the woodcut of a Renaissance-era Caesarean-section birth, Wallace continues to analyze the representation of mothers. Likely intended to depict the achievements of professionalized, masculinized modern medicine (58), the woodcut centers a male doctor holding a long blade and leaning against the cut-open body of a prone woman. Another woman, whom Wallace reads as a midwife, is extracting a baby from the mother's uterine incision while three additional men and three additional women stand on either side of the birthing/operating table. Though Wallace's analysis here is even shorter than her thoughts on Cinderella, she covers a lot of ground. She comments on the division of labour in the image ("crying and sucking are for women" 57) and observes that the image is constructed as if to present "The New Holy Family" that divides women from men through violence. She reads it as a celebration of problematic linear notions of progress and as "a testimony to the triumph of male medicine" (58). What Wallace finds most compelling and infuriating is the disregard for the mother's body, which she links to the denigration of the earth writ large. Whereas in Cinderella Wallace found evidence of the mother's power within the details of the story, here she sees evidence of the longstanding misogyny that denies such power. But because she recognizes the absent presence of maternal power, Wallace's counter-reading turns the woodcut in to "a talisman, a way of retrieving" something from the past (58).

Following a critical response to Sharon Olds' poem, "Bread," in which she finds "no chinks [...]. At all," Wallace closes the series of "readings, meditations" with her poem, "Bones."[5] "Bones" functions effectively as a conclusion to the four reflections. Like the contemplation that begins with the coffee mug, "Bones" presents readings of objects: the mother's shank-turned-weapon and the bones themselves. Like the Cinderella reading, "Bones" depicts protective maternal power. Like the woodcut, "Bones" evokes the field of medicine (shanks, x-rays, CAT-scans) while also conjuring other kinds of knowledge and truths. "Bones" affirms the vulnerability and strength of women's stories and their bones, physical and metaphorical, in contrast to the subjugation of women's bodies that Wallace reads in Olds' poem, and in mainstream readings of the woodcut and Cinderella.[6]

Two Women Talking does not include any direct response from Moure to this April 1986 missive but "Bones" resurfaces in their letters nearly a year later. The Women and Language panel that sparked their correspondence was originally scheduled to take place in 1986 but was pushed to 1987. In February 1987, Wallace sent her prose statement of poetics, "One More Woman Talking," to Moure and indicated, "I'd like to read a poem ('Bones'—I think I sent it to you once?)" (73). In March, she asks that "Bones" be her "statement" in the workshop handout (83) and reiterates this request again in April (90). The final letter in the *Two Women Talking* correspondence is from Moure to Suniti Namjoshi, another panelist, providing an update on the workshop and proceedings.[7] About Wallace, she writes "Bron Wallace withdrew her talk from the booklet and asked for the poem to be printed instead" (91). This is indeed the case in the chapbook that emerged from the panel, *Illegitimate Positions: Women and Language 1987* (Ford and McMaster 41-44).

Eventually, "One More Woman Talking" also made its way to publication. Of course, it is in *Two Women Talking*, which was published after *Illegitimate Positions*, but it also came out in *Sudden Miracles: Eight Women Poets* in 1991 and *New Contexts of Canadian Criticism* in 1996 (Tregebov 237-243; Heble et. al 168-174). In "One More Women Talking," Wallace explicates much of what she demonstrated in the four "readings, meditations" and "Bones." As in the first line of "Bones," a story "got this one going," this time her own story of finding feminist solidarity within the Student Union for Peace Action, a formative moment that Wallace also describes in "Feminists, Like Explorers, Spend Their Lives Venturing Into Unknown Territory" (*AW* 107). She goes on to affirm that her poems are born from "women's stories, women's conversations" (38 *supra*) which she sees as venues that are ideally safe, confident, and loving enough to facilitate women's exploration of their own power.

These comments on power, "that power which is so often belittled or denied by the society around us (or by ourselves)" (38 *supra*) harken back to her analyses of Cinderella and the woodcut. The statement continues with Wallace's thoughts on the challenges of voice in her poetry, the use of "everyday language" and "how to convey this sense of inner discovery at the heart of the most prosaic anecdote" (39 *supra*). Again we see that given the essentialness of voice, stories, and conversation to Wallace's poetics, it is no wonder that she objects to the idea that women have been mute throughout history. The idea of women's speechlessness was put forth in an Xavière Gauthier quote discussed at the Feminist Caucus workshop and which Moure had shared with Wallace in their correspondence (McMaster 68; Ford and McMaster 1).[8] Admittedly, Wallace may be making a strawman of Gauthier's claim; Gauthier's statement about women's muteness could be strategic hyperbole. Nonetheless, the idea of women's historical silence provokes Wallace to articulate her feminist poetic convictions and methodology. To further refute the presumption that women are silenced, Wallace offers the example of her great grandmother, whom she inserts into history by writing about her (40 *supra*).[9] In the context of my seminar, this idea reverberated with Dionne Brand's "No Language Is Neutral," another course text that affirms a writer's capacity to bring mothers and foremothers into the historical record, albeit with struggle. Though from a setting and point of view quite distinct from Wallace's, Brand's speaker states, "History will only hear you if you give birth to a / woman who smoothes starched linen in the wardrobe / drawer, trembles when she walks and who gives birth / to another woman who cries near a river and / vanishes, and who gives birth to a woman who is a / poet, and, even then" (23). For Wallace, the foremother's consequential presence in history does not even ultimately depend on her immortalization in poetry: she argues that even if she had never written about her great grandmother, "regardless of what is recorded," her great grandmother "exists, she persists, she *moves events*" (41 *supra*).

Throughout the next part of "One Woman Talking," Wallace continues to identify and denounce misguided assumptions: that men and women are synonymous with "oppressor / victim," that language is patriarchal and deterministic, that one must adhere to specific language theory to be "theoretically correct" (43 *supra*). As she moves toward the conclusion of her statement, she elaborates on her conviction that change is possible, for people, culture, and language. Her examples emphasize change that comes from quotidian, locatable interventions, which are both pervasive and hard to see—like the cracks through which she saw the coffee cup, Cinderella, and the woodcut with feminist eyes. What changes language, in Wallace's opinion? "A poet who writes a poem that challenges conventional syntax and grammar," certainly, and this is a nod to the feminist language theory that so enlivens Moure (42 *supra*). But Wallace also names "a man who admits he is violent and asks for help," and "Cyndi Lauper singing 'Girls Just Wanna Have Fun,'" and finally "two women sitting in a bar talking to each other" (42 *supra*).[10] Two paragraphs later, her concluding sentence again evokes the importance of women talking: "what matters to me personally is being here, in May, in another room, with another bunch of women, still talking" (43 *supra*).

At the end of our seminar on *Two Women Talking*, the students and I concluded our in-class engagement with the text by creating found poems from their words. We each went back over the text, choosing words and phrases that we found evocative and arranging them creatively. As we all read our poems aloud, phrases of Moure's and Wallace's wound around each other in new configurations, imbibed with each of our own stories on that day. Our closing activity paid homage to Wallace's poetic methodology in a tiny way: we picked up something we had been given and worked with it on the page to see where it led. For Wallace, working with the gifts of "women talking" is fundamental to her poetics, as is the commitment to reading the world subversively, actively—

even stubbornly—for potential change. In the constellation of texts found in *Two Women Talking*, Wallace both explicates and demonstrates these foundational stances in ways that can be read and embraced, this many years later, in conversation.

Notes

1. Critics have commented on what Brenda Vellino calls "the primacy of the conversational, storytelling mode" to Wallace's poetics (98-99 *supra*; see also essays by Lee, Freiwald).

2. Intriguingly, Wallace also describes feminism in these terms: "feminism is a relocation; you take up a new place in the world" (*AW* 109).

3. At the time *Two Women Talking* was published, Erín Moure spelled her name Erin Mouré. This essay uses the current spelling, except in the citations for works published under the previous spelling. For more of Moure's thoughts on Wallace, see her essay, "Deeper Than Any Silence: Bronwen Wallace (1945-1989)" in *My Beloved Wager* (2009) and her poem "Ordinary Cranium," which was reprinted in the *Open Letter* Special Issue on Bronwen Wallace (1991) edited by Rudy Dorscht and Savoy.

4. Lydia, the protagonist in Wallace's story "Chicken 'n' Ribs," also has the capacity to imagine the workers whose labour supplies her food and drink (*PYT* 18, 22) via an international industry that Wallace discusses in her essay "Sugar Plums and Calabashes" (*AW* 121).

5. *Two Women Talking* does not reproduce the Sharon Olds' poem, which is from her collection *The Dead and the Living* (77). A few lines are quoted and it is paraphrased as a poem in which the speaker equates her young daughter with the bread she is baking (59). Wallace wrote critically of Olds earlier in the correspondence as well (18).

6. Although Wallace places "Bones" at the conclusion of the "readings,

meditations" it was not included in the reprinting of *Two Women Talking* found in *Imprints and Casualties: Poets on Women and Language, Reinventing Memory* (Burke).

7. Susan McMaster's introductory "Note to the Reader" explains that they included the letter to Namjoshi as a kind of postscript "to the give reader a sense of how the workshop and panel went, in the event. (Since Erin and Bronwen both attended, they didn't correspond about it.)" (7-8).

8. The full Gauthier quote appears in "One More Woman Talking" (39 *supra*).

9. Wallace is likely referencing her poem "The Family Saints and the Dining-Room Table" (*MF* 53).

10. The example evoking a man is important and connects to Wallace's assertions about the reformative potential of men who commit violent acts (*AW* 23, 143-4). Further, even her larger understanding of voice, story, and conversation is not only about women talking, as she makes clear in her essay "Why I Don't (Always) Write Short Stories" (*AW* 176).

Works Cited

Brand, Dionne. *No Language Is Neutral.* Coach House, 1990.

Burke, Anne, editor. *Imprint and Casualties: Poets on Women and Language, Reinventing Memory.* Broken Jaw, 2000.

Finn, Patrick. "When Editing Goes Write: The Correspondence of Erín Moure and Bronwen Wallace." *Textual Studies in Canada*, vol. 13/14, 2001, pp.101-112.

Ford, Cathy, and Susan McMaster, editors. *Illegitimate Positions: Women and Language 1987.* Feminist Caucus of the League of Canadian Poets, 1992.

Freiwald, Bina. "'This isn't one to be told / in the third person': Wallace's Life-Stories." *Bronwen Wallace*, special issue of *Open Letter*, vol. 7, no. 9, 1991, pp. 112-133.

Heble, Ajay, Donna Palmateer Pennee, and J.R. (Tim) Struthers, editors. *New Contexts of Canadian Criticism*. Broadview, 1997.

Lee, Dennis. "A Geography of Stories." *Bronwen Wallace*, special issue of *Open Letter*, vol. 7, no. 9, 1991, pp. 11-14.

McMaster, Susan, editor. *Two Women Talking: Correspondence 1985 to 1987 Erin Mouré and Bronwen Wallace*. Feminist Caucus of the League of Canadian Poets, 1993.

Moure, Erín. *My Beloved Wager: Essays from a Writing Practice*. NeWest, 2009.

Olds, Sharon. "Bread." *The Dead and the Living*. Knopf, 1983, p. 77.

Rudy Dorscht, Susan and Eric Savoy, editors. *Bronwen Wallace*, special issue of *Open Letter*, vol. 7, no. 9, 1991.

Toews, Miriam. *Women Talking*. Knopf, 2018.

Tregebov, Rhea, editor. *Sudden Miracles: Eight Women Poets*. Second Story, 1991.

Vellino, Brenda. "'A Network of Relations': Ethical Interdependence in Bronwen Wallace's Talking Lyric." *Postmodernism and the Ethical Subject*, Edited by Barbara Gabriel and Suzan Ilcan. McGill-Queen's UP, 2004, pp. 302-332. Revised and reprinted *supra*.

Jeremy Baxter
Remembering in Blue

Blue is the colour of Neptune, Uranus
icy gas spheres spin crystalline
in methane cold rhythms
shaking glass mountains
ringing silent through the universe.

Blue is the scattered colour of the sky
the atmosphere is prejudice
red and yellow light is let through
but blue gets tagged and pulled over for detainment
by surly customs particles
scattered through the ionosphere.

Blue is the jungle river in Mexico
Agua Azul
a blue vein of life slicing
the cool green fern patches
and the jungle-moss earth swallows
the lush blue sounds of life.

Blue is birth—
emerging into air
cold blue transcendence
and blue is brilliant light absorbed
as eyes awaken blue
and new skin opens
after an eternity of warm darkness.

Blue are the eyes of the child
seeing for the first time
the way the world is
beautiful
and full of pain.

Blue are the collars of the working class
and blue is their struggle
for justice
their fists clenched in frustration
wanting to be heard
demanding only what is fair
needing
to be proud and blue.

Blue are the bruises
and the sadness
that time will heal over
though scars will always remain
left over
to remind us
in unexpected moments
when we are alone and blue.

Blue is the woman laughing at the new years eve party
her blue tears of hysterical joy
blue puffs of hot hazy smoke
she is getting drunk and hands gesture
swirling bright blue
eyes closed
beneath the blue warmth of burning skin
and blue is her vibrant energy
that she casually emits

as those around her marvel at this magic
her words flowing neatly into place
capturing the simple beauty
within our lives
she smiles blue
and laughs as the world around her
spins and careens
almost too blue.

And then the sudden cold depths of blue
beneath the empty swirls of night
where blue is the dead colour of a face
silent and dreaming—a frozen expression
so still no one breathes
where every sound hangs
from the dead blue night walls
and the stiff shaking air
and blue is the undertaker moving softly at dawn.

Blue is the swishing sound of souls
from time immemorial
as everyone gathers
together—watching
this unity
a magical blue energy
anxiously waiting
as though for the show to begin.

"Remembering in Blue" from *Common Magic: The Book of the New*. Edited by Elizabeth Greene and Danielle Gugler. Artful Codger, 2008, pp. 79-81. Used with permission.

Wanda Campbell
Selected Bibliography

PRIMARY SOURCES

Poetry

Bread and Chocolate/ Marrying Into the Family. with Mary di Michele. Oberon, 1980.

Signs of the Former Tenant. Oberon, 1983.

Common Magic. Oberon, 1985.

The Stubborn Particulars of Grace. McClelland & Stewart, 1987.

Keep That Candle Burning Bright and Other Poems. Coach House, 1991.

Marrying into the Family. Oberon, 1993.

Collected Poems of Bronwen Wallace. Edited by Carolyn Smart. McGill-Queen's
UP, 2020.

Prose

The Exploitation of Experience: Some Thoughts on the Study of Literature. Hogtown
Press, 1971. 9 pp.

"Women's Lives: Alice Munro." *The Human Elements: Critical Essays.* Edited by
David Helwig. Oberon, 1978, pp. 52-67.

"In Other Words." *Kingston Whig-Standard.* 1987-1988. Columns rpt. in
Arguments with the World: Essays by Bronwen Wallace. Edited by Joanne
Page. Quarry, 1992.

Helwig, Maggie and Bronwen Wallace, editors. *Coming Attractions.* Oberon, 1989.

People You'd Trust Your Life To. 1990. Rpt. with additional story. McClelland &
Stewart, 2001.

Arguments With the World: Essays by Bronwen Wallace. Edited by Joanne Page.
Quarry, 1992.

*Two Women Talking: Correspondence 1985 to 1987 Erin Mouré and Bronwen
Wallace.* Edited by Susan McMaster. Feminist Caucus of the League of
Canadian Poets, 1993.

Translations

Lieu des origines: poèmes choisis, traduits et présentés par Isabelle Miron. Poems translated by Isabelle Miron in collaboration with Éric Bergeron. Noroît, 2016.

Si c'est ça l'amour. Stories translated by René-Daniel Dubois. Les Allusifs, 2017.

Films

All You Have To Do, in collaboration with Chris Whynot (1982)

That's Why I'm Talking, in collaboration with Chris Whynot (1984)

Interviews

Cantar, Brenda. "Interview with Bronwen Wallace." *Arc Magazine*, vol. 20, 1988, pp. 45-54.

Carey, Barbara. "WQ Interview with Bronwen Wallace." *Cross-Canada Writers' Quarterly*, vol. 6, no.4, 1984, pp. 3-4, 29.

Gzowski, Peter. "The Morningside Interviews." *Open Letter*, vol. 7, no. 9, 1991, pp. 15-25. Rpt. in *Arguments With the World: Essays by Bronwen Wallace*. Quarry, 1992.

Meyer, Bruce and Brian O'Riordan. "The Telling of Stories: An Interview with Bronwen Wallace." *Poetry Canada Review* vol. 9, no. 3, 1988, pp. 3-5. Rpt. in *Lives & Works: Interviews by Bruce Meyer and Brian O'Riordan*. Black Moss, 1992, pp. 100-107.

Neschokat, Sylvia. "Politics, Poetry & Patriarchy: Interview with Bronwen Wallace." *The Optimist*, vol. 9, no. 2, June 1983, pp. 5-6.

Vandenbeukel, Fay. "Interview with Bronwen Wallace." *Room of One's Own*, vol. 14, no.1, 1990, pp. 53-63.

Williamson, Janice. "The Landscape from How I See my Poems Moving: An Interview with Bronwen Wallace." *Open Letter*, vol. 7, no. 9, 1991, pp. 26-35. Rpt. in *Arguments With the World: Essays by Bronwen Wallace*. Quarry, 1992, pp. 201-214 and *Sounding Differences: Conversations with Seventeen Canadian Women Writers*. U of Toronto P, 1993, pp. 286-298.

SECONDARY SOURCES

Articles and Book Chapters

Barclay, Adèle. "Commemorating Common Magic." *The Queen's Journal*. 7 March 2008. www.queensjournal.ca/story/2008-03-07/news/commemorating-common-magic/

Baxter, Jeremy. "Remembering in Blue." *Common Magic: The Book of the New.* Edited by Elizabeth Greene and Danielle Gugler. Artful Codger, 2008, pp. 79-81.

Bennett, Donna. "Bronwen Wallace and the Meditative Poem." *Queen's Quarterly*, vol. 98, no. 1, 1991, pp. 58-79.

Billings, Robert. "Contemporary Influences on the Poetry of Mary di Michele." *Contrasts: Comparative Essays on Italian-Canadian Writing*, edited by Joseph Pivato. Guernica, 1985, pp. 121-152.

Burke, Anne, editor. *Imprints and Casualties: Poets On Women and Language, Reinventing Memory*. Broken Jaw, 2000.

Common Magic: *The Legacy of Bronwen Wallace Conference*. Queen's University, March 2008. podcasts.apple.com/us/podcast/common-magic-the-legacy-of-bronwen-wallace /id430628505

Crummey, Michael. "On Winning Inaugural Bronwen Wallace Award." *YouTube*, uploaded by Writers Trust of Canada, 28 July 2014, www.youtube.com/watch?v=MFw1NeOzy5U

di Michele, Mary and Barbara Godard. "'Patterns of Their Own Particular Ceremonies': A Conversation in an Elegiac Mode, between Mary di Michele and Barbara Godard." *Open Letter*, vol. 7, no. 9, 1991, pp. 36-59.

---. Editor. *Anything is Possible: A Selection of Eleven Women Poets*. Mosaic, 1984.

Finn, Patrick. "When Editing Goes Write: The Correspondence of Erin Moure and Bronwen Wallace." *Textual Studies in Canada*, vol. 13/14, 2001, pp.101-112.

Freiwald, Bina. "'This isn't one to be told in the third person': Wallace's Life-Stories." *Open Letter*, vol. 7, no. 9, 1991, pp. 112-133.

Geddes, Gary. "Notes on the Poets: Bronwen Wallace (1945-1989)." *15 Canadian Poets x2*. Oxford UP, 1990, pp. 565-566.

---. "Bronwen Wallace, 1945-1989." *Canadian Literature*, vol. 124-125, Spring 1990, p. 391.

Greene, Elizabeth and Danielle Gugler, editors. *Common Magic: The Book of the New*. Artful Codger, 2008.

Hall, Phil. "Twenty Lost Years." *Killdeer: Essay-Poems*. Book*hug, 2011, pp. 33-48.

Kertzer, J.M. "'The stubborn arguments of the particular.'" *Open Letter*, vol. 7, no. 9, 1991, pp. 71-87.

Kulyk Keefer, Janice. "'Telling Our Grief': Photographic Image in Bronwen Wallace's 'The Scuba Diver in Repose." *Image et Récit: Littérature(s) et arts visuels du Canada*. Presses Sorbonne Nouvelle, 1993, pp. 209-227.

Lahey, Anita. "Poetic Justice." *Walrus*. vol. 17, no. 4, 2020, pp. 61-65.

Lane, Patrick. "For Bronwen Wallace." *Last Water Song*, 2007. Rpt. in The *Collected Poems of Patrick Lane*. Edited by Russell Brown and Donna Bennett. Harbour Publishing, 2011, pp. 455-457.

Laplante, Josée. "Bronwen Wallace: magnifique découverte." Interview with René-Daniel Dubois. *La Presse*. 27 March 2017. https://www.lapresse.ca/arts/livres/201703/27/01-5082682-bronwen-wallace-magnifique-decouverte.php

Lee, Dennis. "Bronwen Wallace's Work Crackled with Energy." *Globe and Mail*, 26 Aug 1989, C18. Rpt. as "A Geography of Stories." *Open Letter*, vol. 7, no. 9, 1991, pp. 11-14.

Martin, Shelley. "Feminism, Motherhood, and Possibilities in the Writing of Bronwen Wallace." *Feminist Mothering*. Edited by Andrea O'Reilly. State U of New York P, 2008, pp.61-72.

McMaster, Susan. "Erin Moure and Bronwen Wallace: from *Two Women Talking: Correspondence 1985 to 1987*." *Quarry*, vol. 42, no. 2, 1993, pp.33-50.

---. and Cathy Ford, editors. *Illegitimate Positions: Women & Language*. Feminist Caucus of the League of Canadian Poets, 1992.

Miron, Isabelle. "La *magie ordinaire* de Bronwen Wallace." *Lieu des origines: poèmes choisis, traduits et présentés par Isabelle Miron*. Noroît, 2016, pp. 7-9.

Moure, Erin. "Deeper Than Any Silence: Bronwen Wallace (1945–1989)." *My Beloved Wager*. Edited by Smaro Kamboureli. NeWest Press, 2009, pp. 41-47.

---. "Bronwen Wallace: De la poésie comme d'une miséricorde." Afterword. *Lieu des origines: poèmes choisis, traduits et présentés par Isabelle Miron*. Noroît, 2016, pp. 91-94.

Nixon-John, Gloria, "Getting the Word Out: The Country of Bronwen Wallace and Emmylou Harris." *The Women of Country Music: A Reader*. Edited by James E. Akenson and Charles K. Wolfe. UP of Kentucky, 2003, pp. 46-60.

Page, Joanne. "Forward." *Arguments with the World: Essays by Bronwen Wallace*. Quarry, 1992, pp. 6-10.

Rudy Dorscht, Susan and Eric Savoy. "Particular Arguments: A Special Issue On Bronwen Wallace." *Open Letter*, vol. 7, no. 9, 1991.

---. "Writing at the Interval." *Open Letter*, vol. 7, no. 9, 1991, pp. 100-111.

Savoy, Eric. "The Antecedents of 'It': A Poetics of Absence." *Open Letter*, vol. 7, no. 9, 1991, pp. 88-99.

Schaub, Danielle. "'A Landmark in Familiar Country': Alcohol in Bronwen Wallace's People You'd Trust Your Life To." *Études Canadiennes/Canadian Studies: Revue Interdisciplinaire des Études Canadiennes en France*, vol. 35, 1993, pp. 231-244.

Scobie, Stephen. "The Voices of Elegy; or, Hurtin' Songs for Bronwen Wallace." *Bolder Flights: Essays on the Canadian Long Poem*. Edited by Frank M. Tierney and Angela Robbeson. U of Ottawa P, 1998, pp. 151-159.

Smart, Carolyn. "A Place at the Table," *Journal of Canadian Poetry*, vol. 5, 1990, pp. 1-2.

---. "Bronwen Wallace: In Memoriam, 1945-1989." *Poetry Canada Review*, vol. 10, no. 3, 1989, pp. 14-15.

---. Editor. *Collected Poems of Bronwen Wallace*. McGill-Queen's UP, 2020.

Tregebov, Rhea. Editor. *Sudden Miracles: Eight Women Poets*. Second Story, 1991.

van Herk, Aritha. "Ghost Narratives: A Haunting." *Open Letter*, vol. 7, no. 9, 1991, pp. 61-70.

Vellino, Brenda Carr. "'A Network of Relations': Ethical Interdependence in Bronwen Wallace's Talking Lyric. *Postmodernism and the Ethical Subject*. Edited by Barbara Gabriel and Suzan Ilcan. McGill-Queen's UP, 2004, pp. 302-332.

Webb, Phyllis. "Bronwen's Earrings." *Hanging Fire*, Coach House, 1990. Rpt. in

"Particular Arguments: A Special Issue On Bronwen Wallace." *Open Letter*, vol. 7, no. 9, 1991 and *Peacock Blue: The Collected Poems*. Edited by John F. Hulcoop. Talonbooks, 2014, p. 417.

Dissertations

Black, Laura. *This Isn't One To Be Told in the Third Person: Social Activism in the Poetry and Prose Writing of Bronwen Wallace*. M.A. Trent University, 2000.

Clinton, Lauren. *Talking Through the Glosa: An Examination of the Conversational Networks Implicit to the Glosa Form*. M.A. McGill University, 2013.

Finlay, Triny. *Intersections: Mapping Genre in the Work of Gwendolyn MacEwen and Bronwen Wallace*. B.A. Mount Allison University, 2000.

Hurlock, Debb. *Cadences of Voice, Conversations of Change: The Poetry of Bronwen Wallace*. M.A. Lakehead University, 1996.

Manley-Tannis, Shelly Lynn. *Dirt-Stained Fingernails: Bronwen Wallace Locating Herself*. M.A. Trent University, 1995.

Moss, Julia. *Changing Levels of Discourse in the Poetry of Robert Kroetsch, Gérald Godin, Bronwen Wallace and Louise Desjardins*. M.A. Université de Sherbrooke, 1993.

Nixon-John, Gloria. *A Place of Rupture: The Life and Poetry of Bronwen Wallace*. Ph. D. Michigan State University, 2001.

Sarson, Paula L. *Telling the Stories of Our Lives: Poetics and Politics in the Works of Bronwen Wallace*. M.A. Dalhousie University, 1993.

Sniderman, Wendy. *Feminist Nostalgia for Healing and Strength: Mnemonic Sites and Signs in Bronwen Wallace's Poetry and Prose*. M.A. Memorial University, 1996.

Reviews

Archer, Anne. Rev. of *Common Magic* by Bronwen Wallace. *Queen's Quarterly*, vol. 93, no. 3, 1986, pp. 663-665.

Atwood, Margaret. Rev. of *Common Magic* by Bronwen Wallace. *Journal of Canadian Poetry*, vol. 2, 1987, pp.120-123.

Boire, Gary. "Arbitrary Magic." Rev. of *Common Magic* by Bronwen Wallace. *Canadian Literature*, vol. 110, 1986, pp. 130-132.

Cantar, Brenda. "The Life You Save May Be Your Own." Rev. of *The Stubborn Particulars* of Grace by Bronwen Wallace. *Arc Magazine*. vol. 20, 1988, pp. 63-68.

Carey, Barbara. Rev. of *The Stubborn Particulars Of Grace* by Bronwen Wallace. *Books in Canada*, vol. 17, no. 2, 1988, p. 31.

di Michele, Mary. "Author's Large-Spirited Feminism Will be Missed." Rev. of *Arguments with the World* by Bronwen Wallace. *The Gazette*. 29 August 1992, J1.

---. "Bronwen Wallace: A Woman You'd Trust Your Life To." Rev. of *People You'd Trust Your Life To* by Bronwen Wallace. *The Gazette.* 14 April 1990, J3.

Dopp, Jamie. Rev. of *Collected Poems of Bronwen Wallace* edited by Carolyn Smart. *Malahat Review*. vol. 214, Spring 2021, p. 105.

Downie, Glen. "Forms for Argument." Rev. of *Arguments with the World* by Bronwen Wallace. *Event*, vol. 22, 1993, pp. 143-147.

Hatch, Ronald B. Rev. of *Common Magic* by Bronwen Wallace. *University of Toronto Quarterly*, vol. 56, no. 1, 1986, p. 35.

---. Rev. of *The Stubborn Particulars Of Grace* by Bronwen Wallace. *University of Toronto Quarterly*, vol. 58, no. 1, 1988, pp. 37-38.

Keefer, Janice Kulyk. "Discoveries and Mysteries." Rev. of *Keep That Candle Burning Bright and Other Poems* by Bronwen Wallace and *Arguments With the World: Essays* edited by Joanne Page. *Canadian Literature*, vol. 138/139, 1993, p. 131-133.

---. Rev. of *The Stubborn Particulars Of Grace* by Bronwen Wallace. *Event*, vol. 17, no. 2, pp. 135-138.

---. Rev. of *People You'd Trust Your Life To* by Bronwen Wallace. *Books in Canada*, vol. 19, no. 5, 1990, pp. 39-40.

Knutson, Susan. Rev. of *People You'd Trust Your Life To* by Bronwen Wallace. *Letters in Canada*, vol. 72, no. 1, 2002/2003, p. 191.

Lepage, Élise. "Poésie." Rev. of *Lieu des origines* by Bronwen Wallace, translated by Isabelle Miron. *University of Toronto Quarterly*, vol. 87, no. 3, 2018, p. 73.

Lockett, Elizabeth. Rev. of *The Stubborn Particulars Of Grace* by Bronwen

Wallace. *Canadian Materials*, vol. 16, no. 5, 1988, p.187.

Lynes, Jeanette. Rev. of *The Stubborn Particulars Of Grace* by Bronwen Wallace. *Canadian Literature*, vol. 122/123, 1989, pp. 212-215.

Moure, Erin. Rev. of *Keep That Candle Burning Bright And Other Poems* by Bronwen Wallace. *Books In Canada*, vol. 20, no. 7, 1991, pp. 40-41.

Robertson, Heather. Rev. of *Arguments with the World: Essays* by Bronwen Wallace edited by Joanne Page. *Books In Canada*, vol. 22, no. 1, 1993, pp. 41-42.

Tregebov, Rhea. Rev. of *Keep That Candle Burning Bright And Other Poems* by Bronwen Wallace. *University of Toronto Quarterly*, vol. 62, no.1, 1992, pp. 67-68.

---. Rev. of *Arguments with the World: Essays by Bronwen Wallace* edited by Joanne Page. *Quill & Quire*, vol. 58, no. 9, 1992, p. 67.

---. Rev. of *Keep That Candle Burning Bright And Other Poems* by Bronwen Wallace. *Quill & Quire*, vol. 57, no.10, 1991, p. 31.

Verduyn, Christl. Rev. of *Arguments with the World: Essays by Bronwen Wallace* edited by Joanne Page. *ESC: English Studies in Canada*, vol. 20, no. 1, 1994, p. 110-112.

Wainwright, J. A. Rev. of *Marrying into the Family* by Bronwen Wallace. *Canadian Literature*, vol. 91, 1981, pp. 148-151.

Whalen, Terry. "Spiritual Autobiographies." Rev. of *Signs of the Former Tenant* by Bronwen Wallace. *Canadian Literature*, vol. 103, 1984, pp. 75-78.

Whitaker, Muriel. "Women Alone." Rev. of *People You'd Trust Your Life To* by Bronwen Wallace. *Canadian Literature*, vol. 132, 1992, pp. 229-230.

Woodcock, George. Rev. of *The Stubborn Particulars Of Grace* by Bronwen Wallace. *Poetry Canada*, vol. 10, no. 2, 1989, pp. 37-42.

York, Lorraine. "Particulars Remembered." Rev. of *Collected Poems of Bronwen Wallace* edited by Carolyn Smart. *Canadian Literature*, vol. 242, 2020, pp.171-172.

Contributor Notes

Jeremy Baxter has worked in Vancouver's arts community for nearly 25 years. He is currently the Technical Director for Théâtre La Seizième, PuSh International Performing Arts Festival, Vancouver International Children's Festival, Vancouver Folk Music Festival, and Vancouver International Dance Festival. He has designed lighting for numerous theatre and dance productions and cofounded Some Assembly Arts Society which creates original theatre productions—written and performed by youth. Jeremy is Bronwen Wallace's son and the executor of her literary estate.

Andrea Beverley is an Associate Professor at Mount Allison University in Sackville, New Brunswick. She is cross-appointed to English and Canadian Studies and is the head of the Canadian Studies program. Her research focuses on Canadian women writers of the 1970s and 1980s, particularly in relation to archives, feminism, and literary collectives.

Wanda Campbell teaches Women's Literature and Creative Writing at Acadia University in Wolfville, Nova Scotia. She has edited *Hidden Rooms: Early Canadian Women Poets* and anthologies for Penguin, and her academic articles and creative works have appeared in journals across Canada. She has also published a novel *Hat Girl* (2013), and five collections of poetry, *Kalamkari and Cordillera* (2017), *Daedalus Had a Daughter* (2011), *Grace* (2009), *Looking for Lucy* (2008), and *Sky Fishing* (1997).

Brenda Cantar is a retired professor of English Language and Literature at the University of Waterloo. Her work was principally in Early Modern poetry and prose and Gender Studies. She was a colleague of Bronwen Wallace at Queen's University at Kingston when Wallace was writer-in-residence and Cantar was completing her doctoral studies.

Mary di Michele, poet, novelist, and member of the collaborative writing group, Yoko's Dogs, is the author of eleven books including selected poems, *Stranger in You*, and the novel, *Tenor of Love*. Her most recent publication is *Bicycle Thieves*, (ECW, 2017). Her awards include the CBC first prize for poetry, the Air Canada Writing Award, and the Malahat Review long poem competition. She teaches at Concordia University in Montreal.

Susan Glickman used to be an English professor, then a creative writing instructor at both Ryerson and the University of Toronto, and now works as a freelance editor. She is the author of seven volumes of poetry, most recently *What We Carry* (2019), seven novels, most recently *The Discovery of Flight* (2018), and one book of literary criticism, *The Picturesque & the Sublime: A Poetics of the Canadian Landscape* (1998).

Phil Hall's book of essay-poems *Killdeer* (2011) won the Governor General's Award, and Ontario's Trillium Book Award. Most recently, Hall has published *Toward A Blacker Ardour* (Beautiful Outlaw, 2020), and *Niagara & Government* (Pedlar, 2020). He is the founder of The Page Lectures series at Queen's University, and lives near Perth, Ontario.

Patrick Lane was born and raised in the hard-scrabble British Columbia interior and his award-winning career as a writer spanned five decades with over twenty collections of poetry, as well novels and nonfiction. *The Collected Poems of Patrick Lane* (2011) contains over 400 poems ranging from *Letters from a Savage Mind* (1966) to *Witness* (2010) and includes the series of elegies that first appeared in *Last Water Song* (2007). He died at the age of 79 in 2019.

Susan Rudy is Director of the Centre for Poetry and an Honorary Senior Research Fellow in the Department of English at Queen Mary University of London. A Professor Emerita of English at the University of Calgary, she is also an Honorary Professor in the School of Literature, Drama, and Creative Writing at the University of East Anglia. Current work appearing in the interdisciplinary international journal *Feminist Theory* focuses on queer women's solidarity, gender ontoformativity, and experimental writing.

Aritha van Herk is the author of five novels, two books of criticism, and many non-fiction and ficto-critical texts, especially works that develop the idea of geographical and historical temperament as tonal accompaniment to landscape. She has published hundreds of articles, reviews and essays on Canadian culture. She teaches literature and Creative Writing in the Department of English at the University of Calgary in Alberta.

Brenda Vellino is an associate professor, teaching in the English and Human Rights departments at Carleton University on unceded Algonquin Anishnaabe territory in Ottawa. She has published on poetry and human rights, as well as on many Canadian women poets, including Dorothy Livesay, Margaret Atwood, Daphne Marlatt, Marlene NourbeSe Philip and Dionne Brand, as well as on Michi Saagiig Nishnaabeg poet, singer, and knowledge keeper Leanne Simpson. Vellino teaches courses and has published on contemporary poetry, contemporary transnational theatre, Indigenous popular genres, Indigenous theatre, and Indigenous human rights.

Phyllis Webb was born in 1927 in Victoria, BC, and worked for many years as a writer and broadcaster for the CBC, where she created the radio program "Ideas" in 1965. Considered a philosophical and feminist poet, before her death in 2021 she authored over twenty books of poetry including *The Vision Tree* (1982) which won the Governor General's Award, *Hanging Fire* (1990) in which "Bronwen's Earrings" first appeared, and *Peacock Blue: The Collected Poems* (Talonbooks 2014).

Lorraine York of the Department of English and Cultural Studies, McMaster University, is the author of *Literary Celebrity in Canada* (2007), *Margaret Atwood and the Labour of Literary Celebrity* (2013), and *Celebrity Cultures in Canada*, co-edited with Katja Lee (2016). Her most recent book, *Reluctant Celebrity* (2018), examines public displays of reluctance as forms of privilege intertwined with race, gender, and sexuality. She has long dreamed of writing a book entitled *Unseemly*, and that's what she's doing now.

Printed in August 2022
by Gauvin Press,
Gatineau, Québec